CHRISTIAN WORSHIP
and its cultural setting

——Frank C. Senn——

FORTRESS PRESS   PHILADELPHIA

Library of Congress Cataloging in Publication Data

Senn, Frank C.
  Christian worship and its cultural setting.

  Bibliography: p.
  Includes index.
  1. Liturgics.   2. Public worship.   3. Christianity
and culture.   I. Title.
  BV176.S45 1983   264   82–48587
  ISBN 0–8006–1700–2

9771J82   Printed in the United States of America   1–1700

CONTENTS

PREFACE

It is an author's happy task to thank those who in one way or another helped to bring a book into being. This particular book is the product of my own need to organize my random thoughts into more systematic reflection. But I have greatly appreciated the encouragement I have received from friends and colleagues to keep on writing, even though I am no longer in a situation where that sort of thing is part of the expectation of my employment. I have carved out time to write from a busy life as parish pastor, father, and husband. I must express gratitude to my wife, Mary Elizabeth, who has tolerated my practice of disappearing during moments of prime-time TV to put down words on paper.

My current occupation is the exercise of the ministry of Word and Sacrament in a vibrant, cross-cultural, pluralistic congregation on the near South Side of Chicago. I could write a book about the vigor and quality of liturgical life at Christ the Mediator Lutheran Church, which existed long before I assumed the pastorate. But instead I have written a book which probes the whole problem of working out a relationship between Christian worship and its cultural setting. This is an issue which has concerned me for a dozen years or so, since I was a graduate student of Aidan Kavanagh in the Liturgical Studies Program of the Theology Department at the University of Notre Dame. This is an opportunity, which I gladly take, to acknowledge the influence and inspiration of Father Kavanagh and my other professors and fellow students at Notre Dame.

The approach of this book reflects the historical and phenomenological approach to liturgical studies which has been emphasized at Notre Dame. This methodology allows the liturgy to speak in its own terms, in the light of its evolution at the hands of those people of God whose "public work" before God and the world it has been. This does not mean bracketing theological and dogmatic questions, but rather letting the concepts and experience of the liturgy itself prompt theological reflection. Only in this way can there be a true liturgical theology.

Since there can be a true liturgical theology that is different, for instance, than systematic theology (which might nevertheless include propositions about the meanings of worship, preaching, and the sacraments within its system), liturgical theology is a discipline that ought to be intentionally included in the curricula of theological seminaries and divinity schools. It is my hope that this book will be of use to seminarians and theology students as well as to pastors and laypersons.

My students at the Lutheran School of Theology at Chicago will recognize in these pages the spirit and sometimes even the letter of my classroom presentations. They should also know that this material has been honed by their probing questions and lively discussions. They did not always agree with me, but their willingness to defend my right to advance such ideas and their warm personal support remains for me a positive aspect of a very trying time in my life. It is therefore with much affection that I dedicate this book to my former students and hope that, as these reflections engage other students, their tribe may increase.

> FRANK C. SENN
> Christ the Mediator Lutheran Church
> Chicago, Illinois
> *In the Great Fifty Days of Easter*
> *1982*

INTRODUCTION

The Relationship of Cult and Culture

The fastest growing Christian churches in the world today are in Africa and Asia. These churches represent the cutting edge of Christian liturgical evolution because they proclaim and celebrate the gospel of Jesus Christ in cultural contexts where the gospel has not yet been incarnated but is perhaps in the process of being so. Consequently a certain cultural schizophrenia characterizes worship in these churches. The sounds of African or Asian instruments, the rhythms of native tunes and dances, and the sight of colorful apparel is juxtaposed with German or English hymnody and with clergy dressed in black gowns or cassocks and surplices. Christian worship will inevitably be adapted to these cultures. Indigenization is necessary to make the gospel relevant to every particular society.[1]

Many Westerners might wonder why the process of indigenization has not occurred faster, especially since vestiges of Western cultural expression in African or Asian worship smack of the legacy of a colonial past. But the issue is not so simple. First, missionaries are not disembodied spirits. They have always brought something of their own culture with them when they evangelized a new territory. Cultural legacies have been cumulative in Christian worship. Thus, our contemporary American Christian worship retains traces of Semitic, Greek, Latin, Romance, Gothic, and Germanic/Anglo-Saxon cultures. Second, the danger of particularization is that it may threaten the universal relevance of the gospel to all cultures. This was precisely the reason Martin Luther was reluctant to give up the use of the Latin rite in favor of an exclusively vernacular one. Particularization can result in a narrow religious provincialism in which the sense of the church's catholicity is lost. Third, it is often necessary to achieve cultural distance in order to effect a complete conversion.

This may be one reason why Charlemagne was anxious to import Roman liturgical books and practices into Frankish territory at a time when entire pagan tribes were being brought into the "Christian empire," admittedly at swordpoint. Is it possible, then, that the use of drums and tribal dances in African worship might evoke latent heathen spiritualities which would undermine Christian doctrine and ethics? Fourth, does indigenization represent the wave of future development in emerging nations? There is no clear consensus about this among native leaders of church and state. Certainly the revival of local tribal or ethnic identity is a way of instilling pride among a people who have been culturally oppressed. On the other hand, the modern communications network is making the whole earth, in Marshall McLuhan's term, a "global village." That network comes in the dress of the Western technocratic culture, and thousands of African and Asian students flock to the colleges and universities of Europe and North America to learn Western technology. Fifth, modern Christian missionaries cannot be faulted for utilizing the commercial avenues and technology developed by the West as a means of facilitating the spread of the gospel any more than the first generation of Christians can be faulted for utilizing Roman trade routes and military highways to spread the gospel around the Mediterranean and Western European worlds.

These musings suggest that the relationship between Christian worship (the cultus) and its cultural setting is complex. It is also the most constant and perennial pastoral liturgical issue. Such a theme may, therefore, suitably serve as a way of organizing this systematic study of Christian worship. Most introductions to worship or liturgical study include basic definitions of worship, a general history of the liturgical tradition, and commentary on individual rites such as baptism and Christian initiation, the Eucharist and the church year, penance and the ministry to the sick, ordination, marriage, burial, and the Liturgy of the Hours.[2] Pastoral liturgics engages in reflection on this basic data with an eye for its application.[3] This present effort falls into that latter category.

The chapters of this book probe Christian worship in terms of the impact culture has had on its evolution and practice. Morphologically, a similarity exists between Christian and non-Christian rites. This was admitted by second- and third-century church fathers, such as Justin Martyr and Clement of Alexandria, who regarded the pagan rites as diabolical imitations of the Christian mysteries. The modern psychologist C. G. Jung would see such ritual acts as washing and eating and drinking as archetypal experiences in all religions and societies. Students of comparative religion, such as Mircea Eliade, have seen parallels between Christian belief and practice and the myths and rituals of other religions and social groups. We will explore these parallels in the first chapter. Such similarities must be taken seriously on theological grounds. The doctrine of the incarnation asserts that the divine Word entered human life in order to redeem it. God communicates with us in terms which are accessible to us; that is the justification for the sacramental life of the church. It should not be surprising, then, that Christian sacramental rites parallel non-Christian ritual practices.

This does not mean, however, that there are no particular forms of Christian worship. In chapter 2 we shall inquire into the theological bases of Christian liturgical forms and trace their historical evolution. But we cannot trace the history of Christian worship without noting the profound contributions which the various cultures, through which it has passed, have made on liturgical form, content, and style. The impact of culture on the Christian cult will be traced in chapter 3.

In chapters 4 and 5 we will take up some large and important ways in which culture affects cultic life—questions of liturgical language and action. We can worship God only in the language we know, and language is conditioned by the vitalities at work in our culture. If we take seriously the communication theories of McLuhan, it would seem that liturgical media today must be more action-oriented. Observers, however, have noted the uneasiness of many worshipers in our society with liturgical actions. Anthropologist Mary Douglas has explored the conditions in society that make ritual behavior possible and the conditions that sustain effervescence. The growth of the neo-evangelical and neo-pentecostal sects suggests a preference for effervescent religion in American society. Can this preference be channeled into forms inherited from the tradition? Some hints will be provided, although this must be left as an open question since each worshiper will respond according to his or her own spiritual needs. But there can be no doubt that liturgy must take on a more active character for the participant if it is really to serve as a vehicle for expressing devotion to God.

In chapter 6 we provide a theological rationale for a more action-

oriented liturgy in which a divine-human encounter takes placé. In
the sacrificial response of the people to God's sacramental action,
expressed par excellence in the eucharistic sacrifice, the very world
itself is offered to God. This can only be the world of culture. Culture
offered to God is culture transformed. This provides a way of viewing
the relationship between cult and culture from a theological perspective: the cult is the agent of the transformation of culture.

The last three chapters spell out some of the ramifications of the
theological convictions articulated in chapter 6. Liturgy is the vehicle
for the people's expression of devotion or piety. It can also serve as
a vehicle for community formation. There are practical ways of doing
liturgy which contribute to both personal and community formation.
When liturgical rites work, for whatever reasons, they achieve genuinely cathartic effects, causing in some cases real transformation of
personal and social relationships.

In the first chapter we provide a definition of cult which, in classical usage, connotes the "cultivating" of relationship with the deity.
This need not imply a manipulation of the deity in the sense of works-
righteousness. Indeed, the Lutheran confessions, which are quite
alert to works-righteous piety, regularly employ the term "cultus" as
a synonym for *Gottesdienst,* "the service of God." It is much more
difficult to provide a definition of culture. We would understand it
in the widest possible sense as "the systematic body of learned behavior which is transmitted from parents to children."[4] This suggests
the cultivation of a whole life style by means of which a society
conceives and enacts its vision of reality and basic values. This vision
and these values may be coterminous with the Christian gospel or at
least informed by the Judeo-Christian tradition, or they may be in
direct or indirect conflict with the gospel. In any event, the vision
of reality and the value systems shared in society daily confront the
worshiper, who will bring them to church. How do pastors and lay
leaders appraise the challenge of the culture in which the Christian
cult is practiced? How do they respond, for example, to the secular
world view which dominates contemporary Western civilization? The
issue of the relationship between cult and culture is one of the major
tasks of pastoral liturgics. The topics taken up in this book seek to
deal with that task. We hope to provide some clarity as we steer a
path between the Scylla and Charybdis of cultural capitulation and
cultural irrelevancy in the ordering and doing of Christian liturgy.

But the reader must be forewarned that some of these issues defy absolute resolution, and many questions must be left open-ended. The hoped-for value of this book is that it will help people appreciate the complexity of the relationship between worship and culture and not give in to simplistic solutions.

Finally, while the Lutheran background of the author will unavoidably protrude in these pages, I have tried to approach the issues from an ecumenical perspective. That approach is aided by the twin factors that the mainline churches transmit a common liturgical tradition, and we must all respond pastorally to the same cultural challenges and opportunities.

the anthropology of WORSHIP

The Role of Myth and Ritual in Human Life

It has been said that some people's ideas of God are too small. As Morton Kelsey reminds us, it is equally true that our view of humanity can be too small. "God has ways of communicating, and the human being has all sorts of depths and capacities for responding, which have been ignored."[1] In the spirit of Jesus, we do not think that people are made for liturgy, but that liturgy is made for people. Yet we have not always taken into account basic patterns of human behavior when discussing or planning worship. We want to begin, therefore, with the observation that human beings have a propensity for transforming the raw stuff of experience into *patterns* that embrace both conceptual structures known as "myth" and behavioral structures known as "ritual."

It is admittedly difficult to use the terms "myth" and "ritual" today. "Myth" is often used popularly to mean something that is untrue. "Ritual" is often used to mean an action that is insincere. Both terms need to be rehabilitated for viable, scientific discourse.

The fact that mythology is studied by students of comparative religion, culture, sociology, psychology, anthropology, and philology suggests that there is something more to it than outright falsehood. The psychologist C. G. Jung has shown the value of taking myth seriously in the lives of people. One of Jung's basic theories was that the collective unconscious—the transpersonal residue in psychic reality—breaks forth in images, symbols, dreams, visions, and myths as a way of expressing experienced reality or human destiny. Jung's conclusion was that people who try to live without symbolic or mythic meaning in their lives tend to incur psychological and physical disorders. It is not surprising that he found more Protestant patients in his office than Roman Catholic or Jewish ones.[2] Protestants have had fewer ways to express primal mythic and symbolic meanings because of their historic aversion to ritualistic ceremonies and customs.

If "myth" is a term that must be rehabilitated for viable use, even more necessary is the rehabilitation of the term "ritual." Anthropologist Mary Douglas observed that "ritual" is often defined as a routinized act diverted from its normal function.[3] Thus, a ritualistic person is judged to be someone who performs certain outward acts which ought to imply an inner commitment to certain values, but who is inwardly uncommitted to those values. The problem then becomes what term to use to describe patterns of behavior which are sincerely performed. We need to use the term "ritual" in a more neutral sense to describe those patterns of behavior by which a social group acts out its values or world view.

Anthropologists have long debated the cause-and-effect relationship between myth and ritual. Does one act first and then supply the meaning? Or does one try to devise actions which express preconceived meanings? Probably both processes may be seen at work in various times and places. At least in the case of the Hellenistic mystery religions, it is now thought that the myth or interpretation was added later by philosophers like Plato to provide explanations of primitive rites whose original meanings were lost. This suggests that a practice which is maintained over a long period of time can receive different interpretations in different periods of history. It is certainly the case that the same action can be interpreted differently in different cultures. Thus, for example, whistling is a form of applause in America but a form of booing in Europe. Or again, the holocaust sacrifice was a horrible rite of aversion to the ancient Greeks but the highest form of adoration to the ancient Hebrews.

Nevertheless, whenever the myth is added to the rite, it does interpret the rite. As Mircea Eliade has noted, the myth is usually in the form of a story which serves as an archetype and is intended to be repeated. It is acted out in the communal rites. This suggests that the disintegration of established patterns of behavior signals the disintegration of accepted values. In an essay published in 1966, Erik Erikson warned that "the decay or perversion of ritual does not create an indifferent emptiness, but a void with explosive possibilities." Perhaps he went on, this "explains why 'nice' people who have lost the gift of imparting values by meaningful ritualization can have children who become (or behave like) juvenile delinquents; and why nice 'churchgoing' nations can so act as to arouse the impression of harboring pervasive murderous intent."[4]

On the other hand, there is a renewing as well as a conserving aspect of ritual action. Ritual has the power to revive experience and perhaps even the values that people once may have had, but have lost. Margaret Mead wrote: "The recurrence of the ritual assures [the participants] that the feeling once was there and may come back again. This is, of course, the principal function of the rituals of family relationships—wedding anniversaries, birthday celebrations, and family reunions—and of all those ceremonies where we attempt to reconstitute ritually a feeling that exists but that may lack any immediate power of expression. It is a . . . function of ritual all over the world."[5]

We cannot solve the problem of the general disintegration of commonly accepted values and modes of expression in our society. We may not be able to solve the problem of the Church's own theological malaise. But we can keep the rituals going and let them accomplish what they may. And as we try to make our liturgical rites as compelling as possible, we can learn much from studies in anthropology and comparative religion. The burden of this chapter is to demonstrate something of what I have learned from these behavioral sciences.

The Characteristics of Cult

Myth and ritual are correlative. Ritual is a pattern of behavior and myth is a pattern of conceptualization. By means of these patterns people try to give a coherent rationale to reality as they have experienced it and to live in accordance with that world view. Myth and ritual are therefore the vehicles by which reality as a whole is transmitted to the members of a society. Together they provide the world view and life style which are the components of cult.

Cult need not be a "religious" phenomenon. Indeed, some of the most gripping cults in modern times have been political cults, such as Marxism, which depends upon the myth of the golden age, and Nazism, which tried to revitalize Teutonic-Nordic mythology. The ritual robustness of these cults can be seen in May Day celebrations in Red Square or *Parteitag* in Nuremberg. The ritual actions in these secular celebrations, like those at a modern American football game, tend to be simple, direct, and aggressive (which might say something to those concerned about liturgical renewal in the churches). Cultic celebrations must make an impression on those who participate in them if what cult communicates is nothing less than reality itself— a world view and life style which is intended to be shared by all the members of the society.

If cultic celebrations provide for an affirmation and enactment of reality as it has been experienced, then this reality must be conceived of socially. It must be capable of being shared by all the members of the society; it must be capable of being adapted in order to deal with the crises that constantly bear upon a community. Aidan Kavanagh has suggested that such a vision of reality must be capable of dealing with the ultimate human threat of death in the form in which each society experiences it. By "death" he includes all the frustrations borne by humans—"from the destruction of a nomad's flocks, through the ruin of agricultural man's crops, on through the desolation of urban man's city, and to the physical cessation of life for them all individually."[6]

Kavanagh notes that societies react against such threats by projecting images of themselves. One such image is that of solidarity with cosmic forces that are superior to the threat. Another image is that of hero extrapolation where one member of the society meets the threat, overcomes it, and rides off into the sunset, leaving the society vicariously purified. Christian views of atonement and redemption depend upon such images. Jesus is proclaimed as one who has overcome the threat of sin, death, and power of the devil. Christians are also able to overcome these threats by identifying with Jesus in his life and death, resurrection and ascension. The difference between Jesus and the pagan hero, of course, is that the pagan hero comes "once upon a time" (in illo tempore). Jesus came at a particular time as a historical person: "when Quirinius was governor of Syria," "in the days of Herod the King." The pagan hero appears from nowhere to leave for realms unknown. Jesus came from the Father and returned to the Father, promising to prepare a place for his own. But the ultimate human threat has been overcome by his own death and resurrection. By ritually reenacting the story of this saving event, the community of believers is also able to overcome the threat.

In Patterns of Comparative Religion, Mircea Eliade stresses that the repetition of the archetypal action serves to abolish time. "By its repetition, the act coincides with its archetype and time is abolished.

We are witnessing, so to speak, the same act that was performed *in illo tempore*, at the dawn of the universe. Thus, by transforming all his physiological acts into ceremonies, primitive man strove to 'pass beyond,' to thrust himself out of time (and change) into eternity."[7] This must be severely qualified when applied to the Jewish and Christian cults because these religions are rooted in unrepeatable historical events rather than in some kind of "myth of eternal return." Yet what Eliade is describing is not unlike the concept of commemoration or *anamnesis* in biblical religion. The language of commemoration or remembrance is transtemporal or sacramental, and in the idiom of this language an event can be "repeated" or reenacted cultically. When Jesus said, "Do this for my remembrance," the kind of "remembrance" he had in mind was not merely a cerebral effort, such as remembering what I did on this day last year. It is an actualization in the present of the saving events of his life and death, resurrection and ascension. The eucharistic memorial is a way by which the faithful become contemporaneous with Christ and the event which took place "on the night in which he was betrayed."

This concept of remembrance as an actualization of past events is most prominent in the Jewish observance of Passover. For more than two millennia, this cultic meal and the educational machinery supporting it have kept alive in the Jewish experience the event of the exodus from Egypt. The repetition of the Passover meal, like the repetition of the Lord's Supper, causes our present observance to coincide with the original. As the head of the household is instructed to say at the Passover Seder by the Haggadah:

> In every generation let each man look on himself
>   as if he came forth from Egypt.
> As it is said: "And thou shalt tell thy son in that day,
>   saying: It is because of that which the Lord did for me
>   when I came forth out of Egypt."
> It was not only our fathers that the Holy One, blessed be he,
>   redeemed, but us as well did he redeem along
>   with them.[8]

The same significance of repetitive commemorations can be seen in secular celebrations as well as in religious ones. One need think only of an old-fashioned Fourth of July celebration in a midwestern town. The speeches recall the events leading to independence, and the listeners are exhorted to persevere in the heritage of liberty.

There is food to be shared picnic-style by the families after the speechmaking (note the connection between word and meal); there are also games and music. At night there is a gala fireworks display and perhaps a pageant reenacting the events leading to the Revolution. The purpose of this celebration is to help the people remember the events of the past, provide a sense of community identity in the sharing of these events, affirm the bond with the founding fathers, and provide the occasion for the rededication of the community to the basic principles for which it stands. This is a liturgical act of civic anamnesis. Were it not for such holiday celebrations and the educational machinery which supports them, important events would remain mere factual data that later generations could read in history books. The celebration keeps alive the events that constituted the community and impresses upon its members the experience of preceeding generations. These celebrations serve to keep the community's identity intact and to insure its continuing existence.

If all this is a true analysis of the meaning, role, and value of cult, then we may draw several important conclusions. The first is that cult is always *social;* it is never individualistic. Even when cultic forms are used privately, that is, apart from the gathering of the communal assembly (*ecclesia*), they remain social in derivation and reference. The Christian who prays alone at home still prays the "*Our Father.*" The ordained minister who performs a baptism in relative privacy, or anoints the sick in a hospital room, or administers Holy Communion to the shut-in members of the parish does so as the appointed representative of the community, and what takes place is the cultus of the church even if no one else is present. But the cultus of the church is expressed par excellence where the *ecclesia* is convened to do its liturgy. *Leitourgia* derives from *lēiton*, "pertaining to the people," and *ergon*, meaning "work" or "service." The term is used variously in the New Testament to refer to the priestly service of Zechariah in the Temple (Luke 1:23), the sacrificial ministry of Christ (Heb. 8:6), the worship of the church (Acts 13:2), and the collecting of money for the poor and suffering saints (2 Cor. 9:12). In these New Testament uses of *leitourgia* the public and social dimensions of cult are exemplified. In its specific Christian use, liturgy is not only public worship but also social action.

Second, cult is *experiential* rather than rationalistic. It deals more in the communal sharing of experience than in the transmission of information. Beliefs and values are most usually communicated in the form of stories and ritual actions. In the Christian cultic gathering, the stories of God's acts of grace and his people's acts of faith are read and commented on. Some of the commentary comes from the Scriptures themselves in the oracles of the prophets and the letters of the apostles. Other commentary comes from contemporary preachers who understand their task to be something different than presenting a theological or ethical lecture. In the ritual actions of washing and eating, the events remembered in the stories are personally applied to and appropriated by individuals in the community. In these sacramental celebrations the objective and subjective character of cultic life is maintained in tension, because, by these means, a history beyond our own invades our history and takes it into its own.

Because cult is experiential, it is also *symbolic.* Symbols speak with primitive power and evoke depths of association which people, separated by time and place, share with each other. Symbols can be ecumenical in ways that signs cannot be because the meanings of symbols are diffuse and imprecise. Nevertheless, the water symbol of baptism appeals to an aboriginal need for cleansing and purification. Eating and drinking in the Lord's Supper employ basic human appetites and means of expressing companionship. Christians share with all people this intuitive way of apprehending reality.

Because cult is experiential and symbolic, Kavanagh suggests that it reaches its highest form of expression in *celebration,* not in propitiation and even less in rational discourse or subjective psychological reflection. This is because at the heart of cultic life is the affirmation of the overcoming of stress and ultimate threat. This is "good news" which results in something more vibrant than discourse or reflection. "Good news" is a trigger to a sense of joy and release, and joy can never be contained; it is always social.

The celebrative character of cult is best manifested in the *festival.* The festival provides the celebrating community with an opportunity for renewal, rejuvenation, re-creation, rebirth. The philosopher Josef Pieper has written that renewal or re-creation is the "fruit of the festival" and that it is "pure gift." It can be prepared for by preparing what is needed and by going through a period of purification, but the essence of the festival can never be planned, organized, or induced. Once the preparations have been taken care of, "no amount of effort, no matter how desperate, can force festivity to yield up its essence."[9]

The celebration of festivals reminds us that cult is finally the dynamic catalyst that produces *culture*—what Kavanagh calls "the continuous and cohesive life-style by which a particular group conceives of and enacts what its values mean."[10] We know that Western language, drama, music, and the arts received impetus for their development from their original use in the Christian cult. Even the seeds of the modern secular culture were sown from the Christian cult with its affirmation that this world and its matter are God's creation and the theater of his grace. Cult and culture stand in a most dependent relationship to one another. As G. K. Chesterton once quipped, only when people had made a holy day for God did they discover they had made a holiday for themselves.

Just as cult is the basis of culture, so worship is the source of doctrine. As the fathers of the church used to say in various ways, *legem credendi lex statuat supplicandi*—"the rule of prayer should establish the rule of belief." Liturgy informs dogma; practice influences profession. In worship the true identity of the church is constituted. The word "orthodoxy" literally means "right praise," not "right doctrine" (from *orthos* and *doxa*). As we confess in the Athanasian Creed, "We *worship* one God in three persons and three persons in one God." The worship of the Father, *through* the Son, *in* the Holy Spirit constitutes the orthodoxy of the Christian church.

Nothing I have said regarding the character of the cult relies on Christian theology for its validation. But all of this has great importance for doing theology. Western Christianity has tended to regard theology as being determinative of worship, to see worship as receiving its form and content from doctrine. As a result, worship has been regarded as an enactment of credal statements *en tableaux*. It has been this no less in Roman Catholic than in Protestant practice since the schism of the sixteenth century. Both Protestants and Roman Catholics have tended to reverse the patristic saying to read, "let the law of belief constitute the law of worship."

It cannot be denied that there is a reciprocal relationship between theology and worship, just as there is between myth and ritual. Nor can it be denied that practices sometimes go awry and lead to undesirable theological consequences. Precisely this unhealthy state of affairs called forth the Reformation in the sixteenth century. Yet from an anthropological point of view, a certain primacy accrues to cultic data; for cult, being social, experiential, symbolic, and celebrative

reaches down through the senses, beyond reason, and lays hold on
a person totally. Cultic data is as wide and as deep as humanity's
own historic awareness of itself and of the world it lives in. For this
reason Christians and Jews have found almost nothing among the
great natural symbols of the world that they have not been able to
assimilate, for this tradition is also populated by real people who
happen to be moved by such things. It is not the task of theology to
sort through these manifold influences to determine which ones are
acceptable and which are not; it is the task of theology to reflect on
cultic data on the basis of the dogmatic tradition in order to establish
for each generation the relationship between the *lex orandi* and the
lex credendi.

Sacraments and Comparative Religion

This phenomenological approach to liturgical studies also has ramifications for sacramental theology. Traditional sacramental theology
has begun with the dominical institutions. But as Louis Bouyer commented in *Rite and Man*, "The fathers did not in the least imagine
that the rite of eating or of washing was a profane action, bare of any
religious significance before Christ's intervention, but upon which he
bestowed a particular meaning by a purely arbitrary decision."[11] On
the contrary, Christ's words of institution provided new interpretations of rites already long-established in the practices of Judaism,
with correlary practices in other religions.

Mircea Eliade has conveniently classified the various rites into
categories concerned with the sanctification of life, the sanctification
of time, and the sanctification of space.[12] Rites having to do with the
sanctification of life are those which deal with moments of crisis or
transition for groups and individuals, such as pregnancy, childbirth,
initiation, marriage, vocation, sickness, death, and burial. These are
rites which we include among the occasional services. Rites which
are repetitive and recurring have to do with the *sanctification of time*.
These include the liturgical cycles of the day, the week, the month,
and the year. They are manifested in liturgies of the word, sacrifices
and sacred meals, agricultural rites, and the like. Rites having to do
with the *sanctification of space* concern taking possession of certain
places and periodically returning to them. The consecration of buildings, anniversaries, homecomings, and pilgrimages fall into this category.

Arnold Van Gennep has compared the basic structure of rites having to do with the sanctification of life with the three phases of a journey: separation, transition, and incorporation. He calls rites of separation from a previous world or status *preliminal*, rites performed during a period of transition or at the threshold of a new world or status *liminal*, and ceremonies of incorporation into a new world or status *post-liminal*. In his classic study of *The Rites of Passage*, he notes that "the life of an individual in any society is a series of passages from one age to another and from one occupation to another."[13] We are not surprised, therefore, to discover that rites of initiation and vocation (for example, baptism, ordination) are the most highly developed rites of passage. These ritual processes stress the liminal, "betwixt and between," stages of transition (for example, the Christian catechumenate, seminary education). Thus, it is not surprising that these rites tend to define the character of the community that performs them because it is in the liminal situation that the bonds of community are formed.

Thus, a place to begin the study of baptism is with the recognition that any society needs to initiate new members into it. Some societies do this better than others, and it is obvious that initiation rites reach their maximal expressions in societies which are relatively stable and where change is bound up with biological processes and meteorological rhythms. This is why anthropologists who study the so-called rites of passage do so among the somewhat secluded tribal societies of Africa, central South America, and Australia. The most developed of these rites concerns the passage from childhood to adulthood, a process which in our society tends to be diffuse and not identified with a single event such as getting a driver's license or graduating from high school. When the child reaches puberty in a tribal society, he is set aside from the rest of the community along with other novices. He is instructed in the myths and rituals of the community. He is tested for readiness to assume adult responsibilities in the society. The rites he undergoes are designed to make an indelible impression and are therefore usually performed on the body (such as circumcision). Such rites are almost always spoken of in terms of new birth; therefore the ordeals of the novitiate involve a death of former ways of life. As Victor Turner points out, "The neophyte may be buried, forced to lie motionless in the posture and direction of customary burial, may be stained black, or may be forced to live for

a while in the company of masked and monstrous mummers repre-
senting, *inter alia*, the dead, or worse still, the undead."[14] In turn,
those who go through such rites are regarded as "blood brothers,"
persons who can be counted on to the death, persons who will bear
their weight in the adult community.

The ancient Christian baptismal practices had many corollaries
with known rites of initiation in world religions, particularly in the
Hellenistic mystery cults. The candidates for baptism were grouped
together in a special class apart from the congregation known as the
catechumenate. They received instruction in the teachings of the
church and were formed into the Christian life style by being engaged
in prayer, fasting, and almsgiving. Note that these are ascetical dis-
ciplines. The purpose of Christian asceticism is simply to organize
life in conformity with the cross of Christ. The purpose of the catechumenate was to help the candidates for baptism put to death their
former way of life (the "old Adam") in order to be born anew into the
life of the Spirit. This period of transition often lasted as long as
three years. There was something about the liminal stage, with its
betwixt and between character, which indicated what the Christian
life between baptismal death and physical death is all about. When
the candidates were declared ready, or "competent," they went
through a series of rites which certainly were intended to make an
indelible impression on them and which were therefore performed on
the body. They were stripped naked, immersed in water, greased
with oil, clothed in a new white garment, and led before the bishop
in the assembled congregation for the laying on of hands as a sign
of their inclusion in the fellowship of the church. For the first time
they participated in the offering of gifts and the eucharistic meal.

The test of "blood brotherhood" was proven many times over in the
early church in acts of martyrdom. Christians rigorously formed by
the catechumenate and robustly initiated into the community of faith
usually did bear their weight in the community. The comparable rigor
of the public penitential rites in the early church indicates that the
baptized *were* expected to live as though they had become new persons in Christ. The structure of these rites shows that those who "fell
from grace" by committing grave sins had to return to the catechumenate to be re-formed in the faith and then to be reassimilated into
the community. In ancient Roman practice the public reconciliation
of the penitents took place on Maundy Thursday. Thus, the periods

of preparation of the catechumens and penitents coincided during the weeks before Easter and gave Lent its enduring character.

Recent revisions of the rites of Christian initiation in several Western churches have aimed at the reintegration of the separated rites of initiation—baptism, confirmation, first Communion—into the unified process that existed in the patristic church and has remained in the Eastern churches. We should note that there are societies in which the rites of initiation are broken up and do not always coincide with puberty. However the rites of initiation are structured, they are designed to culminate in a rite of incorporation into the inner life of the community, which for Christians is first Communion. As Van Gennep notes, "The rite of eating and drinking together . . . is clearly a rite of incorporation, of physical union, and has been called a sacrament of communion."[15] So if first Communion precedes what we have called "confirmation," confirmation may indeed have the character of a rite of passage, but it should not have the character of a rite of initiation. The confirmand is already a member of the community. On the other hand, the practice of the ancient church of concluding Christian initiation with first Communion is shared by many Christians today, who instinctively realize that one is not fully a member of the community until he or she has received all the rights and privileges of membership.

Once initiation has taken place, that which is effected by the rites of initiation must be remembered and renewed. The community periodically comes together to rehearse the communal myth in a liturgy of the word, to offer to the deity, to receive strength from the deity and from one another, and to bind themselves to the deity and to one another. It is not surprising that a common meal often provides the context for such celebrations. It has been suggested that the sacred meal may be the origin of sacrificial rites.[16] Meat is sometimes eaten in these rites so that the participants may gain the vitality of the animal. The blood of the victim also serves to bind together the members of the group. Bread is a primordial symbol of fellowship (note that the word *companion* includes the word *panis* and means "one who shares bread"). Alcohol is often consumed because this is associated with feelings of joy and festivity, the liberation from inhibitions, the numbing of pain, the overcoming of fatigue, and the swearing of loyalty (the toast).

There are many corollaries with the Christian Eucharist in the phenomenology of sacred meals. Certainly the sense of fellowship and shared mission was an important aspect of the meals shared by Jesus and his disciples, of which the Last Supper was the most significant. That Last Supper became a sign-act, proclaiming Jesus' expiatory sacrifice for the forgiveness of sins. The postresurrection meal fellowship was even more significant since the risen Lord was present among his failed disciples, bringing the gift of forgiveness and reconciliation. The meanings of the Lord's Supper are many and varied; certainly this is a dimension with which we must begin and to which, in this life, we must often return.

Phenomenology also has ramifications for pastoral theology. God may use liturgy for the communication of his grace through Word and Sacrament; but liturgy is obviously a human act performed by a human community for the glorification of God and the edification of its members. As a human act, liturgy ought to be *humane*; that is to say, people should be able *to be themselves* in worship. This means that the forms and styles of celebration should be expressive of the indigenous culture.

A subdivision of anthropology known as "ethnography" would be helpful in teaching pastors how to get to know the various social groups with their shared cultures to which they are called to minister.[17] Ethnography is a careful description of a culture in its own terms, usually obtained from firsthand accounts. The value of such studies to pastors is that they would help those who tend to move from one social group (parish) to another to come to know and appreciate the shared world view and behavioral practices of the local group. It would be hazardous to make precipitous liturgical changes before the shared culture of the social group is reckoned with. It is important for pastors to realize that every social group takes its own culture for granted. People always think the way they do things is natural and the way other people do things is strange. So one cannot just import practices from one parish to another. This might seem to militate against any kind of social change; yet that is not the case. What adds to the complexity of analysis is that there is frequently more than one cultural perspective for any given social situation. Especially in a complex society, such as ours in North America, perspectives differ on various issues depending upon one's social position, occupation or profession, economic situation, age or sex. A pastor is likely to find in any parish those who will support certain changes. And the phenomenological method we have employed in this chapter indicates that the range of symbolic syntax a people is capable of articulating is considerable. Of course, the method is descriptive rather than prescriptive. A pastor will have to know his or her people in order to judge what kind of symbols will speak to them in their own cultural milieu. But phenomenology has demonstrated the universality of many symbols, and this suggests that one need not be timid in exposing people to a broader range of ritual experience.

This may seem like walking on a tightrope. On the one hand, we say, "Know your people and their shared view of reality and behavioral practices." On the other hand, we say, "There is a fundamental commonality to human experience and perception." There is no easy way out of this kind of tension. In the next chapter, however, we will provide some hints as to what ought to be stable and continuous in Christian liturgical practice and where there can be areas of flexibility and openness to indigenous cultural expression. If we can determine how rites have evolved in the history of the church, we may have some clues as to how they are evolving today—often right under our noses.

2

the form of WORSHIP

Theological Considerations of Liturgical Form

If what we do in worship is a corporate endeavor, then some kind of order is necessary so that everyone knows what is happening and is able to participate fully. People put themselves into something confidently only when they know what they are doing. Wherever there is interaction between people, ritual forms and ceremonies arise, whereby the bonds between them can be symbolically expressed. Ritual thus provides a pattern of communication and behavior which is foundational for social intercourse. What I mean by "pattern" is the repetition of human activities which seek to reduce the seemingly random stuff of experience to manageable proportions. Ritualization is not an attempt to escape from reality; it is an attempt to deal with reality as it is encountered, but with some degree of coherence.

Among the reformers, Luther was most appreciative of liturgical form and order. His study of the Bible, especially the Old Testament, convinced him that there could be no public worship without form and order. In an extended discourse on ceremonies appended to his 1520 Commentary on Psalm 14, he pointed out the necessity of the ceremonial in the courts of kings and in the worship of God.[1] This sensitivity to the psychological necessity of ritual forms explains in part Luther's hostility to liturgical innovation and improvisation. In his treatise on the *Formula Missae et Communionis* (1523), he states that he got involved in the work of liturgical reform partly to combat those "fickle and fastidious spirits who rush in like unclean swine without faith or reason, and who delight only in novelty and tire of it as quickly, when it has worn off."[2] In his *German Mass*, Luther warned against those liturgical renewalists who felt obliged to produce a new order of worship just when the people had gotten used to the old one. He felt that true worship and meaningful instruction were impossible if there were no established forms in which these things could be done.

The necessity of liturgical form is further dictated by the circumstance that Christians come together to hear the Word of God proclaimed and to share the eucharistic meal. The reading of Scripture and preaching necessitates that someone rise to speak while others listen. The celebration of Holy Communion also necessitates that someone distribute the elements to those who receive them. These two constitutive acts of Christian worship raise the problem of order. From earliest times the problem of who is to preach and who is to preside at the Lord's Supper has been solved by the institution of a special ministry of Word and Sacrament. This ministry has taken different forms and different names throughout the ages, but its existence in the church has not been questioned.

We should also note that the existence of this ordained ministry in the church does not preclude members of the assembly from offering or praying alone or ensemble. Moreover, every prayer that is offered and every act of proclamation must be affirmed by the congregation; hence the use of the word "Amen." That mode of praying was already practiced in the apostolic era. The doxological conclusion of the Lord's Prayer, found in some later manuscripts of Matthew's Gospel, indicates that even the Lord's Prayer was probably recited by an individual (for example, the presiding minister) and was then concluded with a doxology spoken or sung by the congregation. It is only a very recent idea that everybody in the assembly must say everything. People were usually given short acclamations, such as "Amen," "Lord, have mercy," or "Come, Lord Jesus," rather than extended orations, because long texts cannot be used with any vitality if everyone is saying them in unison. From time immemorial, it has been found better to have long texts sung if they are to be employed in unison by the whole congregation. This also facilitated memorization of texts before the invention of the printing press and the realization of widespread education.

Thus, there are some restrictions placed on the forms of worship by the very character of the church's worship as a corporate activity. But there are also restrictions placed on the forms of worship by the character of the church as the eschatological body of Christ. Because the church is a human institution, forms are inevitable. However, because the church is also a divine institution living in eschatological freedom, forms cannot be absolutized. Details of the forms of worship can have nothing to do with salvation. This represents the other side of Luther. He was adamant against binding people's consciences with liturgical forms. So pervasive was the liturgical legalism of the late Middle Ages that Luther was constrained to warn against the legalistic adoption of even his own liturgical forms. Throughout his *German Mass* he kept insisting that the work was not to be used as liturgical legislation or as a snare for consciences. And once it no longer served a useful purpose, it was to be discarded. Moreover, the circumstances and conditions of congregations were so varied that it was not even possible to legislate an order of worship that would be relevant to every gathering of God's people. The Augsburg Confession emphasizes that "for the true unity of the church *it is enough* to agree concerning the teaching of the Gospel and the administration of the sacraments. It is not necessary that human traditions or rites and ceremonies, instituted by men, should be alike everywhere" (Article VII).

What has been instituted by men may be used with some degree of indifference. But what has been commanded by Christ cannot be a matter of indifference. First, the Word must be preached. This means that readings from the prophetic and apostolic writings of sacred Scripture will be read and expounded in the worshiping assembly. The forms of proclamation may vary from age to age, from place to place, and from preacher to preacher, but the Word must be proclaimed. Second, Holy Communion must be celebrated by the congregation in conformity with Christ's institution. What must be done under the divine command can be summed up as follows: with prayer and thanksgiving, the Lord Jesus and his instituting meal must be commemorated—bread and wine must be consecrated, distributed, eaten, and drunk. However, the way in which this is to be done is not fixed. There is not even a prescribed form of the institution narrative because there are variances in all four biblical accounts of the institution of the Lord's Supper. In addition, the words of institution have been augmented, decreased, or harmonized in various historical church usages. Despite these variances the Word must be preached and the sacraments must be celebrated (even these two constitutive elements of Christian worship admit to manifold possibilities of form). All else is left to liberty of usage, and the areas open for freedom of liturgical expression are, therefore, very great.

There are, however, at least two factors which abridge liturgical freedom. One is concern for the weaker brethren; the other is respect for the historical tradition. With regard to the weaker brethren, love remembers its responsibility not to encumber the conscience of the brother. What might be done in evangelical freedom—in terms of retaining traditional usages or discarding them—is left undone if the brother's conscience is thereby offended and his faith weakened. This is one of the reasons for the gradual character of liturgical reform in the Lutheran Reformation. Another reason, however, was respect for the tradition. Decisions have been made in the history of the church which only *schwärmei* or fanatics can afford to disregard or ignore. The church does not exist just for today. It also exists *with* the company of the saints who have served God throughout the ages. This obligates the church at all times to approach with critical respect those traditions which do not conflict with Christ's institution and the Holy Scriptures as the norm of faith and practice. It is because we live in eschatological freedom that we are also free to *accept* those forms of worship which have endured the test of time. These forms are symbols, but so are doctrines. Liturgical and doctrinal symbols coalesce when considered concretely and historically. The creeds of the church, for example, have been called "symbols." They have functioned theologically to crystalize and demarcate the faith of the church; but they have also functioned liturgically to provide for the personal profession of faith (as the Apostles' Creed is so used in baptism) and to rehearse and transmit the faith from one generation to another (as the Nicene Creed has been so used in the eucharistic liturgy).

For these reasons various reformers have recognized their responsibility sometimes *not* to exercise Christian liberty—especially if radical changes will cause a crisis of faith—even though these reformers perceive a gap between current practices and the practices of the "early church," between recent tradition and the long tradition, between theological understanding and popular piety.

One example which caused much concern during the Reformation was the elevation of the host and chalice at the consecration of the

Sacrament. This practice began during the thirteenth century as a devout visible proclamation of the presence of Christ in the sacrament. It was attended by the ringing of bells and genuflection. It was the high moment of the Mass for many of the faithful, and understandably many superstitious ideas clustered around it. But Luther was able to distinguish between the act itself and popular interpretations attached to it. Therefore, in his *Formula Missae* of 1523, Luther recommended the retention of the elevation for the sake of the weaker brethren who might be offended if it were suddenly abolished. By the time he prepared the *German Mass* he was ready to provide a different interpretation for this symbolic act. He suggested that the elevation be retained "because it goes well with the German Sanctus and signifies that Christ has commanded us to remember him."[3] The elevation thus served as a kind of action sermon. A few years later Luther found another reason for retaining it: it served as a profession of faith against those who denied the real presence.[4] It was a way of expressing adoration of and exciting faith in the real presence of Christ in the Sacrament. For this reason the elevation was retained in many Lutheran churches long after it was abolished in the Reformed churches. It was not abolished in Wittenberg until 1542; but in Sweden it was practiced until 1595.

The Lutheran Reformation understood the deep psychological need people have for established forms and ritual patterns. It tended to prefer variations in form determined not by the subjective whims and fancies of liturgical leaders but by the objective commemoration of the redeeming work of Christ, as that is expressed in the church year. True Christian subjectivity was seen as a personal appropriation of the objective act of God in Christ, which the liturgical tradition proclaims with such clarity. The Western liturgy, even more than the Eastern liturgy, has a built-in principle of variation in the Scripture readings, propers, customs, and ceremonies of the church year. Luther indicates his preference to retain the church year with its festivals and seasons in both his *Formula Missae* and his *German Mass*. The Augsburg Confession, Article XV, clearly indicates the Lutheran reverence for the received liturgical tradition: "Our churches teach that those rites should be observed which can be observed without sin and which contribute to peace and good order in the church. Such are certain holy days, festivals, and the like."[5]

Elements of Liturgical Form: Synagogue and Table

What form was evangelical worship to take? The reformers were somewhat familiar with the Greek Rite and the liturgical teachings of some of the Greek fathers. They could cite these sources, and often did, in support of their doctrinal and liturgical positions. They knew from their limited historical awareness that there has been some amount of variety in the forms of worship down through the centuries. They could even point to the various missal and breviary traditions of the ecclesiastical provinces and religious orders in the Western church as a sign of variety of usage, even though the underlying shape of the liturgy was the same. It was this basic shape to which Luther, Zwingli, Bucer, Calvin, and Cranmer turned in their liturgical revisions, some of the reformers retaining more of the secondary and tertiary accretions than the others.

This basic shape of the liturgy is recognizable already in the description of Christian worship provided by Justin Martyr in his *First Apology* (ca. 150), chapter 67. Even today the order which Justin describes is still discernible in different Christian traditions, both Eastern and Western. If any form of worship may lay claim to ancient and ecumenical character, it is the one which follows this order:

1. Readings from the Scriptures (which Justin calls "the memoirs of the apostles" and "the writings of the prophets")
2. Homily or sermon by the "president"
3. Common prayers
4. Kiss of peace
5. Presentation of bread and wine
6. Thanksgiving by the president, with congregational "Amen"
7. Distribution of the elements by the deacons

Even the Liturgy of Holy Baptism could be drawn into this order, as Justin indicates in chapter 65 of the *First Apology* and as the ancient Liturgy of the Easter Vigil demonstrates.

This order of worship may be divided into two parts: the Liturgy of the Word (also called the Ante-Communion, the Pro-Anaphora, and the *Missa Catechumenorum*) and the Liturgy of the Eucharistic Meal (also called the Holy Communion, the Lord's Supper, and the *Missa Fidelium*). The basic shape of this Liturgy of Word and Sacrament, already sketched out in Justin's account, was solidly established by the fourth century. The Liturgy of the Word consisted of readings from Scripture, psalmody, preaching, and intercessory prayer. It was open to all, baptized and unbaptized alike. The Liturgy of the Eucharistic Meal (the Mass of the Faithful) was the special privilege of the baptized. Catechumens, penitents, and other unbaptized persons were dismissed before the Eucharist began with the offering of gifts.

In the East, where the Western custom of a daily Eucharist never became common practice, the Pro-Anaphora was the principal daily service. There is also evidence, for example, in Egeria's description of worship in Jerusalem in the late fourth century, that the Eucharist could be celebrated without the Liturgy of the Word. But the combined Liturgy of Word and Sacrament was clearly the normal Sunday worship of Christians.

It is becoming increasingly clear that the roots of these Christian services are found in Jewish worship. The Pro-Anaphora is rooted in the synagogue service; hence it has also been called *synaxis*, or "gathering." The church took over from the synagogue the customs of reading portions of Scripture (pericopes) in sequence, of expository preaching, and intercessory prayer. The great prayer of the synagogue was known as *Shemoneh 'esreh* (The Eighteen Benedictions), or simple *Tefillah* ("the prayer"), or *Amidah* ("standing"). The prayer was read by the leader (the *hazzan*), but the people punctuated the petitions with their "Amens." The "Amen" found early entree into Christian worship, as later did the "Alleluia" (derived from the *Hallel*, or "praise" psalms). One important element in the synagogue which did not come into Christian worship was the daily recitation of the *Shema*, "Hear, O Israel . . .". C. W. Dugmore has suggested that this was because the Romans forbade the Jews to recite the *Shema* in public, and by the time they were again allowed to recite the *Shema* publicly, christological theory had advanced to such a degree that Christians could not recite it without a denial of the preeminent place held by Christ.[6]

The origins of the Eucharist have been much debated. Was the Last Supper a Passover Seder? The synoptic Gospels say that it was, but the Fourth Gospel places the crucifixion of Jesus on the day of preparation when the lambs were sacrificed in the Temple.[7] It probably suffices to say that the Last Supper was celebrated in a Passover atmosphere. Early Christian interpretation of the Lord's Supper is loaded with paschal allusions, but the content of the Passover meal has not been continued in Christian usage. Instead, the broken loaf at the beginning of the meal and the shared cup at the end of the meal have become the focus of attention because of the words of Christ concerning them.

The prayers of blessing which Jesus recited over the bread and cup belong to a genre known as *Berakah*, or "blessing." The meal *berakoth* can be seen in the Mishnah.[8] The prayers known as the *kiddush* were recited before the meal over the first cup and the bread; a series of *berakoth* known as the *Birkat ha-mazon* was recited at the end of the meal over the final "cup of blessing." Texts of the Passover *berakoth* can be found in a ninth-century A.D. liturgical collection known as the *Seder Rav Amram Gaon*.[9] While this seems like a late date, it should be remembered that except for the Qumran discoveries we have no copy of the Hebrew Bible before this time. Moreover, Christianized versions of these meal prayers can be seen in chapters 9 and 10 of the *Didache*, a church manual dating from the beginning of the second century A.D. Because this is the earliest collection of Christian liturgical materials, we will want to look at it in greater detail. It provides clear evidence that the form of the Jewish meal *berakoth*, especially the thanksgiving after the meal, evolved into the Christian eucharistic prayer.

The *kiddush* prayers, as found in the Mishnah, are as follows:[10]

> Blessed art Thou, O Lord our God, King of the universe, who createst the fruit of the vine.

> Blessed art Thou, O Lord our God, King of the universe, who bringest forth bread from the earth.

The first two prayers in chapter 9 of the *Didache* correspond to these prayers:

> We give thanks to thee, our Father, for the holy vine of David thy servant, whom thou didst make known to us through Jesus thy servant; to thee be glory forever.

> We give thanks to thee, our Father, for the life and knowledge which thou didst make known to us through Jesus thy servant; to thee be glory forever.

The Jewish table prayers have been spiritualized in the *Didache*. The "fruit of the vine" becomes the "holy vine of David," a symbol of the church. The *Didache* does not mention the bread at all. The only reason we know that the second prayer was spoken over the bread is because of the rubric that precedes it—"And concerning the broken bread." The visible object of the Jewish blessing, the gift of earthly produce, has been transformed into a thanksgiving for the invisible spiritual gifts of "life and knowledge."

The third prayer in chapter 9 of the *Didache* seems to be based on an idea common in a number of Jewish prayers.[11] The *Didache* prayer is:

> As this broken bread was scattered on the top of the mountains and gathered together became one, so let Thy Church be gathered together from the ends of the earth into Thy Kingdom: for thine is the glory and the power through Jesus Christ forever.

Among Jewish prayers which express the theme of gathering the dispersion are the tenth benediction (*Qibbus galuyoth*) from the *Amidah* of the synagogue service:

> Blow the great horn for our liberation, and lift a banner to gather our exiles. Blessed art Thou, O Lord, who gatherest the dispersion of Thy people Israel.

the blessing preceding the *Shema*:

> Let peace come over us from the four corners of the earth and cause us soon to go upright to our land, for Thou hast chosen us from all peoples and tongues and hast brought us near unto Thy great name in love.

and the *mussaf* prayer from the *Yom Kippur* Liturgy:

> Unite our dispersion from the midst of the nations, and gather our dispersion from the ends of the earth, and lead us back into Zion your city.

The *Didache* sees the unity of the many in the shared loaf. This was a popular idea in the early church, and it found expression in the Syrian and Egyptian liturgical sources of the fourth century.

Chapter 10 of the *Didache* is modeled on the Jewish thanksgiving after meals, the *Birkat ha-mazon*. The Jewish grace consisted of four blessings, but the fourth was not added until after 135 C.E. Since the compiler of the *Didache* did not use it, it has been suggested that he did not know it. The Jewish blessings express thanksgiving for the gifts of creation, for the signs of election, and end with a supplication for the fulfillment of promise. The content of the second and third blessings was often determined by the festival on which they were used. We will compare here the ordinary meal *berakoth* with their Christian equivalents.[12]

Birkat ha-mazon	*Didache*
Blessed art Thou, O Lord, our God, King of the universe, who feedest the whole world with goodness, with grace and with mercy. Blessed art Thou, O Lord, who feedest all.	We give thanks to Thee, holy Father, for Thy holy Name, which Thou hast caused to dwell in our hearts and for the knowledge and faith and immortality which Thou has made known to us through Jesus thy servant. To Thee be glory forever.
We thank Thee, O Lord our God, that Thou hast caused us to inherit a goodly and pleasant land, the covenant, the Torah, life and food. For all these things we thank Thee and praise Thy Name forever and ever. Blessed art Thou, O Lord, for the land and for the food.	Thou, Lord Almighty, didst create all things for Thy Name's sake; both food and drink Thou didst give to men for enjoyment, in order that they might give thanks to Thee, but to us Thou hast graciously given spiritual food and eternal life through Thy servant. Before all things we give thanks to Thee that Thou art mighty: To Thee be glory forever.
Have mercy, O Lord our God, on Thy people Israel, and on Thy city Jerusalem, and on Thy Temple and Thy dwelling place and on Zion Thy resting place, and on the great and holy sanctuary over which Thy Name was called, and the kingdom of the dynasty of David mayest Thou restore to its place in our days, and build Jerusalem soon. Blessed art Thou, O Lord, who buildest Jerusalem.	Remember, O Lord, Thy Church, to deliver her from every evil, and make it perfect in Thy love, and gather it from the four winds, it, the sanctified, into thy kingdom which Thou has prepared for it. For Thine is the power and the glory forever.

It is obvious that the Jewish blessings have freely been adapted to Christian use. The benefits of election in the second Jewish blessing have been transferred to the first prayer in the *Didache*: "the knowledge and faith and immortality which Thou hast made known to us through Jesus Thy servant." It is the second prayer in the *Didache* which refers to the food. This suggests that the theme of creation has been subordinated to the theme of redemption, which became a common pattern in classical eucharistic prayers, including the proper prefaces in the Roman eucharistic tradition with their christological motifs. The prayer for the restoration of Jerusalem in the third Jewish blessing has become a supplication for the church in the *Didache*.

There is no anamnesis-proper in the *Didache*, and not surprisingly there is no institution narrative. The institution narrative found a place in the eucharistic prayer only when a formal anamnesis was included. "Do this in remembrance of me" became a dominical warrant for doing the commemoration. This is why there is an institution narrative in the Anaphora of Hippolytus (ca. A.D. 217) which has an anamnesis, but probably not in the third-century East Syrian Anaphora of Addai and Mari which lacks a clear anamnesis.[13] There is no epiclesis in the *Didache* either, but Jean Daniélou has suggested that the invocation of the "holy Name" is a reference to the *shekinah*, or presence of God, tabernacling among us and is therefore a precursor of the epiclesis.[14] In this light some liturgical theologians in the twentieth century have viewed the whole eucharistic prayer as a consecratory epiclesis, which enables us to move beyond the scholastic concern to pinpoint a particular "moment of consecration."

The eucharistic pattern which emerged from these Jewish roots includes the praise of God for his work of creation, the remembrance of his redemptive acts, and supplication for the benefits of communion. The act of praise was expanded with the Sanctus (derived from the *qedushah* of the *berakoth* preceding the *Shema*); the remembrance was brought into specific focus by the inclusion of the institution narrative (similar narrative embolisms have been noted in the second and third parts of the *Birkat ha-mazon* for certain holy days); and the supplication was concretized with the invocation of the Holy Spirit. This liturgical-theological synthesis is best seen in the West Syrian anaphoras of the *Apostolic Constitutions*, Book VIII, St. James of Jerusalem, St. Basil, and St. John Chrysostom. Recent research, however, has suggested that the Roman Canon actually represents an older bipartite pattern of praise/supplication, such as we see in the Anaphora of Addai and Mari, if we take the Sanctus as a demarcation between the two major sections.[15] This would account for the profusion of the sacrifice motif and the commemorations and intercessions through the post-Sanctus section of the Canon.

The eucharistic prayer is, of course, only one element in the meal liturgy. So one other issue with which we must deal is how the eucharistic liturgy evolved as a whole into the form in which we know it today. Gregory Dix proposed the brilliant thesis that the New Testament institution narratives relate not only a Gospel tradition, but also a liturgical order.[16] There are variations in detail in the four institution texts, but the *sequence of actions* is invariable. Jesus (1) took bread, (2) gave thanks over it, (3) broke it, (4) gave it to his disciples, (5) took the cup after supper, (6) gave thanks over it, and (7) handed it to his disciples—seven actions in all. Dix postulated that at the point when the Lord's Supper was separated from the context of a community meal, these seven actions were fused into four:

1. The offertory—bread and wine are placed on the table together;
2. The consecration—the presiding minister gives thanks over the bread and cup;
3. The fraction—the bread is broken;
4. The communion—the bread and cup are distributed together.

These elements of the eucharistic liturgy were enclosed between the greeting of peace before the offertory in the non-Roman liturgies (in the Roman rite the greeting of peace is located before the Holy Communion), and a post-communion prayer and dismissal afterward.

As we said, the basic shape of the liturgy was established by the fourth century. From this point on the unified Liturgy of Word and Sacrament evolved along similar lines in different families of rites. At the end of the patristic period we may differentiate five ritual families: the East Syrian (Liturgy of Addai and Mari); the West Syrian (*Apostolic Constitutions*, Book VIII, and the Liturgies of St. James of Jerusalem, St. Basil, and St. John Chrysostom); the Egyptian Liturgy of St. Mark; the Roman Mass (with similar rites in North Africa and Milan); and the Gallican-Hispanic-Celtic rites. The two families which have been most historically prominent are the Roman and the Byzantine. It is instructive to see how these liturgies developed in response to similar stimuli.[17]

Both liturgies acquired elaborate entrance rites to cover the entrance of the clergy into the magnificent basilicas built for Christian worship after the Edict of Milan in 313, which gave legal status to the Christian cult. Entrance rite material included psalmody (introits and antiphons), the litany prayer known as the *Kyrie eleison*, and a song of praise (*Trisagion* in the Byzantine liturgy and *Gloria in ex-*

celsis in the Roman). It is generally believed that the Roman liturgy was influenced by the Byzantine as regards the liturgical material, but the model for both liturgies was imperial court ceremony. The Scripture readings were interspersed with meditative psalmody (the Gradual) and the Alleluia heralding the Gospel. Choral material was added to cover action during the offertory and communion processions. By the eighth and ninth centuries, however, material of a more dubious nature was entering both liturgies as a product of an increasingly affective devotion and a greater sense of awe in the presence of the sacred mystery. This included private prayers said by the celebrant at the offertory and before the Holy Communion. A whole preparation rite for the celebrant and his assistants developed, first in the East (the *Proskomidia*), and then in the West. The preparatory office included devotions for the celebrant, prayers for each vestment while vesting (which allegorized the meaning of each vestment), and the preparation of the gifts in the East and the preparation of the ministers in the West (including the prayers of confession and for absolution, the *Confiteor* and *Misercatur*). On the other hand, some ancient elements fell out of the eucharistic liturgy during the Middle Ages, such as the Old Testament reading and the responsorial psalm, the prayers of the faithful in the West, and the kiss of peace. An interesting survival in the Byzantine liturgy was the dismissal of the catechumens before the liturgy of the faithful well after the time when there were actually catechumens to be dismissed. Such survivals, however, while not immediately relevant to the situation of the worshiping community, remind that community of what might be relevant in changed circumstances.

Liturgical form in the West was further affected by the Reformation in the sixteenth century. Again we may differentiate various families of rites: a conservative revising of the inherited rites by the Lutherans and Anglicans; an effort to take inherited patterns and conform them to what were perceived to be biblical patterns and materials by the Reformed communities of Switzerland and the Rhineland; and a more radical effort to repristinate New Testament worship by the Anabaptists.[18] The mutual influences of various Protestant rites on one another help to delineate some of the characteristics of Protestant worship. The Anglican Prayer Books show the influences of both Lutheran and Reformed church orders from the continent. Lutheran influence on the Prayer Books of King Edward VI (1549 and 1552) derives primarily from the fact that the Archbishop of Canterbury, Thomas Cranmer, turned to such sources as the Brandenburg-Nürnberg (1533), Mark Brandenburg (1540), and Cologne (1543) Church Orders for models of the revision of prayer texts that were common to both English and German medieval missal and breviary traditions. In fact, the Cologne Church Order, which had been prepared jointly by Philip Melanchthon and Martin Bucer at the request of the Archbishop of Cologne Hermann von Wied was translated into English in 1547 (revised 1548) and published under the title *A Simple and Religious Consultation*. Like its Lutheran models the 1549 Prayer Book retained the outline of the medieval Mass and the propers for the church year. It departs from those models by locating the congregational confession of sins and absolution just before the distribution of communion instead of before the beginning of the Mass, and by providing a long canon which was an evangelical rewriting of the Roman Canon whereas the Lutheran Mass-orders generally reduced the consecration to the Preface, Words of Institution, and Sanctus.

While some Reformed influence is discernible in the 1549 Prayer Book, it is much more evident in the 1552 Prayer Book, especially in such aspects as the rehearsal of the Ten Commandments in the introductory rite, the placing of the communion table in the midst of the chancel, and the phrasing of the words of distribution of the bread and cup so as to avoid any suggestion of an oral eating and drinking of the body and blood of Christ ("Take and eate this, in remembraunce that Christ dyed for thee, and feede on him in thy hearte by fayth, with thanksgeuing"). The Elizabethan Prayer Book of 1559 merged the distribution formularies of the 1549 and 1552 Prayer Books, making possible an articulation of the real presence.

English Puritans who found the *Book of Common Prayer* unacceptable moved to the Netherlands. There they were influenced not only by Calvinist but also by Anabaptist practices, the latter eschewing any kind of fixed prayer formularies. The Puritan Separatists (Congregationalists) brought these forms of worship to New England.[19] The Puritan patterns of worship generated the "Free Church" tradition, which includes the Baptists, Disciples of Christ, and Churches of Christ. The Free Church tradition has also influenced the Presbyterians and Methodists, who are originally related to the Reformed and Anglican traditions, respectively. The Puritan Order of Worship described in John Cotton's *The True Constitution of a Particular Visible Church Proved by Scripture* (London, 1642) included opening prayers of thanksgiving and intercession, the singing of psalms, reading and expounding and preaching the Word of God (there was no reading of Scripture without commentary), exhorting the congregation and questioning of the preacher by the laity, and then "celebrating" the Lord's Supper "once a month at least." The communion liturgy was led by elders sitting at the table. It literally followed the seven actions recorded in the New Testament institution narratives, which meant that the bread and cup were blessed and distributed separately by deacons to the communicants sitting in their seats (non-communicants having been dismissed). The service ended with the singing of a psalm, a blessing, and dismissal of the congregation.

What is noteworthy in comparing ritual orders as diverse as Eastern Orthodox, Roman Catholic, Lutheran and Anglican, Reformed and Free Church, is their basic structural agreement: introductory rite, proclamation of the Word, intercessions, presentation and blessing of the bread and wine, communion, and dismissal. While the homily has been reinstated in Roman Catholic masses, most Protestant churches are moving toward the ideal of weekly celebration of the Lord's Supper. The "return to the sources," which has characterized the efforts of modern liturgical revision, has resulted in the revised liturgies of the Roman Catholic, Anglican, Lutheran, Presbyterian, and Methodist Churches sharing similar characteristics: the restoration of three biblical readings with a common church year calendar and three-year lectionary, psalm singing between the readings, litanized intercessions, the enacted greeting of peace, offertory procession with bread and wine and other gifts of the people, and a plethora of eucharistic prayers. There is common agreement that the eucharistic prayer should say what needs to be said about the eucharistic rite, but there are so many meanings associated with the Lord's Supper that one fixed prayer cannot articulate them all. Thus, the reformed *Roman Sacramentary*, the *Book of Common Prayer*, and the *Lutheran Book of Worship* (Ministers Edition) each have four prayers; a Methodist supplementary worship resource entitled *At the Lord's Table* provides no fewer than twenty-two Great Thanksgivings. There is even considerable ecumenical agreement on the structure of the eucharistic prayer. It includes introductory dialogue, proper preface or general act of praise, Sanctus, recital of salvation history and/or preliminary epiclesis, institution narrative, anamnesis-oblation, epiclesis, intercession, concluding doxology, and "Amen." These ritual forms presuppose and express certain doctrinal convictions, but practice also influences profession. Convergence and consensus in practice, therefore, bodes well for Christian unity and the resolution of historical theological differences.

Changes in Liturgical Form:
Christian Initiation as an Example

Just as the Christian liturgies of the Word and the eucharistic meal derive, respectively, from Jewish synagogue and table liturgies, so Christian baptism is probably a development of Jewish lustration rites. The ministry of John the Baptist was very likely modeled on the kind of ritual washings practiced by the Qumran community, but it expressed repentance for the remission of sins in preparation for the coming reign of God (Mark 1:1f.). Jesus submitted to John's baptism as a sign of the inauguration of his own messianic ministry, and it is reasonable to suppose that the form of Christian baptism was derived from John's. However, the content of Christian baptism was much richer. It was not just the forgiveness of sins; it was also a sign of dying with Christ in order to share in his resurrection (Romans 6). Paul's contrasts of the old life with the new life in Christ, or the life of the flesh with the life of the Spirit, are based on baptism. The Fourth Gospel alludes to baptism by water and the Spirit (John 3:5; 7:38f.). In 1 John we also have reference to the *chrisma*, the anointing of the Spirit (2:20; 2:27). The "water and the blood" of 1 John 5:6–12 has been interpreted as referring to baptism and the Eucharist,[20] although the "blood" could also refer to martyrdom. There are several episodes in Acts which describe baptisms. These have an ambiguous quality because sometimes the gift of the Spirit follows baptism (2:38; 19:5f.), sometimes it precedes baptism (10:44–48), and sometimes it occurs without any immediate connection to baptism (18:25). It is clear that for Luke it is the gift of the Holy Spirit which makes a person a Christian. Thus, the Samaritan converts are not really Christians until the Spirit comes upon them when the apostles lay on hands (8:4ff.). The embryonic elements of a baptismal rite in the New Testament would include some kind of preparation, expressed through repentance; dipping in water, with mention of the name of Jesus or the name of the Trinity; and possibly anointing, or the laying on of hands, or both.

In the postapostolic literature these elements become more stable. From brief passages in the *Didache* and in the *First Apology* of Justin Martyr we see that preparation for baptism includes fasting and moral instruction. The threefold form of baptismal interrogation has become standard. As the candidate assents to each question, he or she is dipped in the water. These questions, as we see from Justin, are the beginnings of the baptismal creed. Baptism leads immediately to the Eucharist. In Justin's *Apology* (chap. 65) it is clear that after the baptism the candidate is introduced to the congregation and for the first time joins in the intercessory prayers, participates in the greeting of peace, and shares in the eucharistic meal. These second-century sources do not mention anointing or the laying on of hands, but this silence is no proof that such actions were unknown.[21]

In the *Apostolic Tradition* of St. Hippolytus of Rome (early third century) we have the earliest description of the full process of Christian initiation as it was emerging in the ancient church.[22] The period of preparation has been expanded to three years for most candidates. This catechumenate included practice in the exercise of ministry (prayer, fasting, almsgiving) and moral instruction. It guided the catechumen over the hurdle of changing his or her life style (and Hippolytus includes a whole list of professions which would have to be renounced and given up before one could become a candidate for baptism). On the night of the *pasch* the bishop met the candidates, prayed for them, and exorcised them. The night was spent in vigil, listening to readings and instruction. At cockcrow the bishop led the "seekers" to the baptistery, a room separate from the eucharistic banquet hall, usually with a sunken pool and a source of flowing water. The bishop blessed the water and the oil which would be used in the rite. The candidates removed their clothing ("Let no one go down to the water having any alien object with them," said Hippolytus). Following the renunciation of Satan and all his service and works, and the first anointing, the candidates went down into the font for the triple profession of faith and the triple dipping in water: little children first ("And if they can answer for themselves, let them answer. But if they cannot, let their parents answer or someone from their family"), then the grown men, and lastly the women. (The Syrian *Apostolic Constitutions* from the fourth century specifies that a deaconess shall baptize the women!)

Following the baptism the candidates come up from the font. They are anointed a second time, put on their clothes, and are led into the assembly before the bishop who lays his hands on them and invokes the gift of the Holy Spirit. Then they are anointed "with holy oil in God the Father Almighty and Christ Jesus and the Holy Ghost." Following the intercessory prayers, the neophytes exchange the kiss of peace for the first time with the congregation, and the deacons bring the eucharistic elements to the bishop. These elements include cups of water and milk and honey for the newly baptized to symbolize inner purification and the neophytes' entrance into the promised land.

The structure of the initiatory process described by Hippolytus remained basically unchanged during the fourth and fifth centuries, although it was greatly expanded and infused with some concepts derived from the mystery cults such as the *disciplina arcani*, the "secret discipline" of withholding certain texts and knowledge until after the initiation. The evidence for the practice of Christian initiation during this post-Nicene period is ample. It is prescribed in church orders and discussed in the mystagogic sermons preached by the bishops to the newly baptized during the week after Easter in order to explain the sacramental rites which they had just experienced.[23]

An issue of special interest is to see how this unified process of initiation disintegrated, especially in the medieval West.[24] We want to note especially the dislocations in initiatory practice that have brought us to our present situation.

First, by the end of the ancient period infant baptism was the prevailing practice. There was no point in conducting a long, instruction-laden catechumenate for infants who could not receive the instruction. The period of the catechumenate was shortened to the Lenten season, and it consisted mostly of prayers of exorcism and blessings performed on the infants. By the high Middle Ages, especially in areas far removed from traditionalist Rome, the catechumenate survived only in ceremonies performed at the church door before the actual baptism. After a long series of exorcisms the candidate was taken into the church while the verse "The Lord preserve thy going in and thy coming out from this time forth and forevermore" was said. At the font there took place the renunciation of Satan, the credal interrogation, the prebaptismal anointing, the baptism, the chrismation, and the giving of a white garment and a lighted candle. This was the order which Luther knew and which he slightly revised in his first *Taufbüchlein* (Baptismal Booklet) of 1523.[25]

Second, the Roman practice was that the bishop personally participate in Christian initiation. The principal role of the bishop was the imposition of hands, invocation of the Holy Spirit, and "sealing" with oil. This practice was adopted in the Gallican church along with other Roman practices during the reign of Charlemagne. While it worked fairly well in central Italy where bishops were plentiful, the relatively small number of bishops overseeing geographically extensive dioceses in trans-Alpine Europe could not be present at every baptismal celebration. So the episcopal, postbaptismal ceremonies were deferred until the child could be brought to the bishop or until the bishop made a visitation to the parish. Consequently, these ceremonies associated with the bestowal of the Holy Spirit, which were called "confirmation" in the West, became separated from the baptismal celebration itself.

Third, the high infant mortality rate in the early Middle Ages, combined with the influence of Augustine's doctrine of original sin, prompted parents to rush their children to the font as quickly after birth as possible. The shortening of the interval between birth and baptism had as its corollary the lengthening of the interval between baptism and confirmation. While the possibility of infant confirmation remained throughout the Middle Ages, by the thirteenth century councils were declaring that infants under the age of seven were too young to be confirmed. The primary reason for this was that the Fourth Lateran Council in 1215 had decreed that every Christian should make confession and receive absolution before receiving Holy Communion. When confirmation was separated from baptism by many years, theologians had to provide a rationale for the rite which would encourage parents to see that their children were confirmed. A common early medieval interpretation was that confirmation was a strengthening of the gift of the Spirit given in baptism to enable the Christian to wage spiritual warfare against the world, the flesh, and the devil. When Thomas Aquinas interpreted the celebrated phrase *augmentum praestat ad gratium* as "growth in grace" rather than as "supplies an addition of grace," the understanding of confirmation as a kind of Christian maturity rite was established.[26]

Fourth, the communion of children at their baptism became problematic with the growing eucharistic realism of the West during the Middle Ages. There was increasing concern about desecrating consecrated elements. Realizing that infants could not swallow the bread, theologians like William of Champeaux appealed to the doctrine of concomitance, which held that the communicant receives the entire Christ under either species. The bread might be withheld from infants but, said William in 1121, "the chalice must be given to them, because, as it is impossible for anybody to enter into life without baptism, so it is impossible without this life-giving *viaticum.*"[27] But scrupulosity about handling the consecrated elements was leading to a growing disinclination to permit any of the laity to receive the cup for fear of spilling the precious blood in its transmission. The removal of the cup from lay communicants effectively ended infant communion. Sometimes infants continued to receive blessed bread and wine, but not the consecrated sacrament. In reaction to this practice, with its possibility of confusing the laity, councils and synods began to decree that infants did not need to receive the Sacrament of the Altar until they reached an "age of discretion." As we have seen, Lateran IV defined this as about age seven when children would be old enough to make confession. We should note in passing that Lateran IV's decree that Christians should go to confession before receiving Holy Communion left an abiding influence on Western eucharistic piety and may be the principal reason for the penitential atmosphere which has surrounded the celebration of the Lord's Supper.

The results of these dislocations were that baptism was not always celebrated in an ecclesial context and came to be viewed as an event which concerned primarily the immediate family. The separation of the Spirit-moment from the water-bath brought confirmation into competition with baptism; the separation of first Communion from Christian initiation created an uncertainty as to what one is initiated into; and the whole process was severed from its paschal roots.

The reformers who rediscovered justification by faith also rediscovered the premier place of baptism in Christian life. All of the reformers were concerned to unclutter the medieval rites and to curb superstition. Accordingly, they rendered the order of baptism into the vernacular, focused on the dominical institution, the confession of faith, and the application of water, and abandoned what they considered to be extraneous and superstitious ceremonies such as the blessing of the font and the use of oil, candles, salt, and spittle. A good deal of biblical imagery was lost in the process, which contributed to the reduction of baptismal meaning in the post-Reformation period. For example, the images of the flood, the Exodus, the crossing of the Jordan, and the baptism of Jesus (which Luther retained in his *Sintflutgebet*, or "flood prayer") connected baptism in the church with its types in salvation history. The loss of the baptismal *Heilsgeschichte* contributed to the privatizing of baptism, and, in the culture Christianity of the Age of Rationalism, baptism was regarded as little more than a name-giving ceremony.

Luther also would have preferred to abandon confirmation, which he regarded as so much *Affenspiel* ("monkey business"). Instead, he envisioned a lifelong catechesis in which children would be admitted to Holy Communion with their families when the pastor judged them ready. But in reaction to Anabaptist charges of spiritual laxity in the Reformation churches, Martin Bucer introduced a rite of public examination of children, who had been baptized in infancy, before they were admitted to Holy Communion.[28] Thus, the evangelical rite of confirmation came to be seen as a gateway to the fellowship of the altar. Among the reformers, Bucer was especially concerned to restore the liturgical practices of the ancient church. He encouraged the celebration of baptism at the celebration of the Eucharist on Sundays and holy days. He was aware that in previous times baptized children also received communion; but this awareness conflicted with his humanist concern that children should be old enough to understand the mysteries of Christ before they are confirmed. Thus, the age of confirmation and first Communion was much older in emerging Protestantism than it had been in the medieval church.

The subsequent history of Christian initiation in German Protestantism saw confirmation acquire preeminence over baptism in pastoral teaching and popular perception. The pietists viewed confirmation as a moment in which those baptized in infancy could make a *personal* profession of faith. Some even emphasized making the confession of faith in one's own words rather than using the words of the Creed. In the culture Christianity of the Age of Rationalism, confirmation was regarded as entrance into the membership of a particular church whereas baptism admitted one into the membership of the general Christian fellowship. Thus confirmation bestowed the rights and privileges of church membership and, along with this, the responsibilities of citizenship. Confirmation was timed to coincide with graduation from elementary school and was sometimes seen as a preparation for apprenticeship, employment, or higher education for boys and marriage for girls. Under such a weight, it is no wonder that confirmation eclipsed baptism in importance.

The progressive dechristianization of Western society during the nineteenth and twentieth centuries under the impact of industrial, political, and social revolutions has made the role of conscious commitment more crucial in the church's practice of making Christians. In a "post-Christian" society, the church can no longer depend on its members to become Christians through cultural osmosis. The Reformed theologians Emil Brunner and Karl Barth even called for an abandonment of the practice of infant baptism in the interests of eliciting from church members a more personal Christian discipleship. While the catholic churches would be loath to abandon infant baptism because it would contribute to a depleting rather than an enriching of baptismal meaning, it is clear that the policy of indiscriminate baptism inherited from the Age of Christendom is no longer tenable.[29] It has been widely recognized that initiation practices must more clearly ritualize separation from the world and incorporation into the church. The Roman Catholic Rite of Christian Initiation of Adults (1972) has tried to do this by restoring a catechumenate of sufficient duration and intensity as to effect conversion.[30]

Recent revisions of the rites of Christian initiation have aimed at restoring the unity of sacramental initiation. Thus, the imposition of hands, invocation of the Holy Spirit, and anointing with oil have been restored in the new Lutheran Liturgy of Holy Baptism.[31] What has been called "confirmation" is now placed, along with the reception of members from other denominations and restoration to membership, under the single title "Affirmation of Baptism."[32] This same pattern is seen in the new *Book of Common Prayer* of the Episcopal Church and the Methodist "alternate text" for *Baptism, Confirmation, and Renewal* (1976). There are those in several denominations who have advocated the communion of all the baptized at the time of their baptism, regardless of age.[33] This would include the communion of infants at their baptism and perhaps thereafter when they seem ready to participate in Holy Communion with their family on a regular basis. The impetus for this practice stems not just from what some might regard as an archaizing tendency among modern liturgists, but also from the impact of developmental psychology, which has given us a richer understanding of infancy and childhood. From such studies as those of Erik Erikson we can appreciate the importance of developing behavioral habits and an ethos conducive to faith formation from a very early age.[34]

Recent changes in Christian initiation, like previous changes, are a response to social and cultural changes, which present the community of faith with new challenges and new opportunities. The church cannot operate in a non-Christian or a post-Christian culture in the same way as it operated in the so-called Christian culture of the Age of Christendom. It is clear that pastoral liturgics must deal above all with the relationship between cult and culture.

3

the culture of WORSHIP

Cult and Culture in the History of Liturgy

The history of Christian worship is the story of the give and take between cult and culture. As the gospel was preached in different times and places, missionaries brought with them the forms and styles of worship with which they were familiar. In time the local people found ways of indigenizing the imported liturgy by infusing it with their own ways of doing things and their own means of expression. When their own culture changed in response to various historical, social, economic, and political factors, liturgical change was not far behind. This is because every generation of Christians has been concerned that its worship be relevant, at least to them.

The question of relevancy is especially vexing during periods of cultural transition when the threat of change drives worshipers either to the experience of dissipation as a result of too much flexibility or to the mentality of rigidity in an effort to find security in the fluctuations of life. The study of the history of liturgy is important in helping us discover what remains essentially the same in Christian worship from one generation to another and what changes as a result of cultural adaptation (*aggiornamento*). Basically what remains the same are the structures or shapes of the liturgy. What changes are the styles of celebration and the kind of devotional elements which flesh out the basic outlines of the rites. The science of liturgiology has done much of its work in the past one hundred years by comparing the structure and historical development of one rite with another. The more recent application of the methods and insights of cultural anthropology has brought out the remarkable degree of similarity in human responses to stress situations as people find refuge in and (wittingly or unwittingly) adapt their traditional rites and symbols in order to meet their current needs.

The basic forms of Christian worship developed from comparable forms of Jewish worship such as the synagogue service, the meal graces, proselyte baptism, the great annual festivals, the weekly Sabbath assembly, and the daily gatherings for common prayer. From these emerged the Christian liturgies of the Word, the eucharistic meal, baptism, the festivals of Easter and Pentecost, the weekly gathering of the whole community on the Lord's Day (but sometimes on the Sabbath as well as among Jewish Christians), and the pivotal daily prayer offices of lauds and vespers. The basic shape of the chief liturgy is already described in the Book of Acts, where it is recorded that the newly baptized "devoted themselves to the apostles' teaching and fellowship, to the breaking of bread and the prayers"(Acts 2:42).

On the other hand, many historical and cultural influences affected the expansion of this simple rite of word, prayer, and meal. That basic shape is the same whether one is reading the description of Christian worship in Justin Martyr's *First Apology* (ca. 150), or the description of the pontifical station mass in *Ordo Romanus Primus* (ca. 700). But the *way* in which the liturgy is done differs considerably from one description to the other, even though both are presumably descriptions of the Roman liturgy. The style of worship has been adapted to meet the very different cultural needs of the second and the seventh centuries.

Cultural adaptation is as old as Christianity itself. If liturgy got stuck in one particular culture, it would be condemned to cultural irrelevancy. To some extent, Jewish liturgy already provided a model for cultural adaptation since it had to meet the needs of Jews in the early common era who lived in Palestine and in the centers of the Diaspora, and who spoke Aramaic as well as Greek. We have seen that a number of Aramaic and even Hebrew expressions have survived in Christian worship to the present day. But Christian worship flourished chiefly in the Greek language in the Mediterranean world, since this was the most universal language in the Roman Empire. Even in the city of Rome itself Christians worshiped in Greek until the middle of the third century. The style of Greek rhetoric, therefore, also left a lasting mark on Christian liturgical texts.

Perhaps one reason for the tenacity of Jewish forms in Christian worship is the antagonism displayed by many Christians toward the culture of classical antiquity. To be sure, there were those apologists of the second century such as Justin Martyr, Clement of Alexandria, and Origen who tried to build bridges between Christian revelation and Greek philosophy. But a more typical attitude was the kind displayed by Tertullian of Carthage who asked, *Quid Athenae Hierosolymis?* ("What has Athens to do with Jerusalem?"). The relationship between the Christian cult and classical culture in the first three centuries A.D. would have to be described, in H. Richard Niebuhr's term, as "Christ against culture."[1] Indeed, one could hardly expect it to be anything else during a time of intermittent persecution. The Roman state was not a friend, but an enemy. Indeed, in spite of two centuries of unparalleled peace and domestic prosperity, Tertullian could say, *Regnum Caesaris regnum diaboli* ("The reign of Caesar is the reign of the devil").

This had its liturgical consequences not only in the fact that private homes were used for worship rather than public buildings, but more especially in the disciplinary structures of the church seen in the three-year catechumenate described by Hippolytus of Rome in his *Apostolic Tradition* and in the comparable *ordo poenitentium* ("order of penitents") described by Tertullian in his *De Poenitentia* (both ca. 200). Hippolytus described a number of crafts and professions a convert would have to give up in order to become a catechumen (obviously pimps, charioteers, gladiators, priests of idols, but also craftsmen who make idols together with actors, soldiers, and magistrates). The purpose of the catechumenate was to help converts across the hurdle of changing their whole way of life from one oriented to "this world" to one oriented to "the world to come" before they entered the waters of baptism. If Christians committed a grave sin after baptism (such as apostacy, murder, or adultery) they had to be reformed in the process of *exomologesis* (public penance) which entailed excommunication, ascetical practices, and reconciliation.

This rigorous discipline was understandably relaxed after the Edict of Milan in 313, which gave Christianity status as a legal cult in the Roman Empire. Now the church had to build bridges to the pagan culture. As a result the practices of the popular mystery cults were sometimes employed by the church in its cult. Many of the new Christians interpreted the Christian mystery as salvation *from* the world, in the character of Hellenistic mystery religions, rather than as salvation *of* the world. Pagan notions of the dichotomy between sacred and profane found their way into Christian spirituality. Church buildings thus became shrines of the deity rather than assembly halls;

the landmarks of the life of Jesus in the Holy Land attracted pilgrims to the splendid shrines erected by the family of the Emperor Constantine; the cult of the martyrs was severed from its eucharistic and eschatological context, and the martyrs were appealed to as heavenly intercessors; and the liturgy became more and more a sacred act performed by professional holy men on behalf of their devotees. As Alexander Schmemann has written, in the process of replacing the old religions, Christianity became a religion; the church as a public institution took on the functions of a religion in terms of providing "the sanction, defense, and justification of all those aspects of the world, society, and life from which it had been cut off during the epoch of persecution."[2]

The increasing attention given by the church to the sanctification of life especially affected such rites of passage as marriage and burial. Roman betrothal practices and the funeral *refrigerium* were adapted and transformed in Christian weddings and funerals. But the attention given to the sanctification of time also contributed greatly to the development of the divine office and the church year. The whole life of Christ was marked out by commemorative celebrations. A number of festivals were forcibly borrowed from paganism as a way of competing with pagan celebrations, most notably the festival of Christ's nativity, which was assigned to the winter solstice since this was the date of the nativity of the *Sol Invictus* (the "Invincible Sun") whom Emperor Marcus Aurelius had proclaimed to be the protector of the empire. Josef Jungmann provides a number of more recondite examples.[3]

It is evident that in the Age of Constantine and in the "Christian Empire" which emerged under Theodosius, the style of liturgical celebration underwent considerable change. Larger congregations necessitated bigger buildings; bigger buildings necessitated a more elaborate choreography just to move clergy and people through the great basilicas. The bishops were invested in the garb and insignia of the senatorial class. Even when styles of clothing changed from the flowing garments of the Romans to the short tunics of the Goths, the clergy continued to wear the old-fashioned clothing in worship. By the sixth or seventh centuries there grew the custom of keeping a special set of garments in the sacristy to put on over one's street clothing. Once this was done the concept of "vestment" was born. It should be noted, however, that the practice of wearing special clothes to mark special occasions is, culturally, nearly universal. Also, the ordinary dress of the formative period of a religion tends to become standard clerical vesture. This principle is seen not only in the survival of alb, stole, and chasuble from the ancient period, and the cassock, surplice, and cope from the medieval period, but also the so-called Geneva gown of the Reformed church from the Reformation period. The black gown was just clerical streetwear in the sixteenth century.

Further cultural adaptation occurred in the Western church when the Roman liturgy was imported into the territories of the Carolingian Empire at the request of Pepin and Charlemagne, who saw in Roman law and ritual a vehicle for bringing order into their unruly realm. The result was not a supplanting of the Gallican rite with the Roman, but a fusion of the two. In such collections of prayers as Alcuin of York's Supplement to the Sacramentary sent by Pope Hadrian I, we have the hybrid origin of the medieval Latin liturgy. The various seventh- and eighth-century sacramentaries have been studied in order to distinguish in them pure Roman material from Gallican.[4] In the conclusion of a seminal essay in this field of investigation, Edmund Bishop wrote: "If I had to indicate in two or three words only the main characteristics which go to make up the genius of the Roman rite, I should say that those characteristics were essentially soberness and sense."[5] It has been observed that the classical Romans preferred matter-of-factness in their speech and dignity in their actions. In contrast, the Franks were willing to engage in a greater excess of emotion, which manifested itself in affective prayers and dramatic ceremonies.

There were plenty of reasons why Western Europe in the period between ca. 700 and ca. 1050 should turn to Rome for a sense of security. The land itself was thinly populated, heavily forested, and largely uncultivated, resulting in commercial atrophy, poverty, and famine. Political structures were largely unreliable and enemies were all around. To the south were aggressive Moslems whose advance into Europe was halted at the Pyrenees by Charles Martel in 732; to the east were warlike Huns and Slavs; and to the north were plundering Vikings. There is little wonder that so many found the contemplative life of the Benedictine monasteries so appealing. At the same time, the monasteries maintained a link with the more tranquil past of classical antiquity. Nevertheless, the world view of the Western European peoples was considerably different than that of classical antiquity. These people viewed reality more empirically; lost on them was the Platonic notion that the spiritual is the real. This change of perspective is perhaps best seen in the carnal realism of the eucharistic theology developing in Western Europe in the early Middle Ages. In the debates between Paschasius Radbertus and Ratramnus of Corbie in the ninth century, it was apparent that symbol and truth (*figura et veritas*), sacrament and reality (*sacramentum et res*), could no longer be held together. These people wanted to *see* reality.

Certainly one reason for the increasing emphasis on the visual in the Western Christian cult was the rise of new vernacular languages between the eighth and tenth centuries and the retention of Latin as a liturgical language. With the rise of new vernaculars, Latin became a specialized hieratic language used by the clergy. There is little wonder that worship took on more visual and dramatic qualities in the sincere effort to make it meaningful to ordinary people. Yet we must be cautious not to make too much of this argument because, in the same period of time, missionaries from Constantinople were translating the Greek liturgy into other vernaculars. Cyril and Methodius in the ninth century actually invented a Slavonic alphabet in order to render the Bible and the liturgy into the speech of the Slavs. Yet the visual is an important aspect of Orthodox worship, especially in the use of icons. But the theology of icons stresses that the picture is a representation of the word, because "the Word was made flesh." Essentially, the icon is a form of visual proclamation of the abiding presence of Christ and his saints in the worshiping assembly. The icons thus help to bridge the gap between the earthly and the heavenly, which is the ambiguous area in which Christian worship takes place. But the Western church, with a greater emphasis on the incarnation and the humanity of Christ, expanded iconography into more lifelike, three-dimensional forms and liturgical symbolism into chancel drama.

These developments in the Western medieval cult made a lasting contribution to Western culture. The dramatic qualities of worship (seen, for example, in the rites of Holy Week which act out the passion story) led to chancel dramas, which constitute the origins of Western theater. The Middle Ages were also a time of the construction of great abbey and cathedral churches, which provided an opportunity for the development of the plastic arts in terms of sculpture and stained glass. The musical requirement of solemn liturgies also provided the impetus for the development of music theory and composition. If the period is called "Gothic," this is because it is the coming of age of the culture of the Goths, the people who had moved into the territories of the ancient Roman Empire in the West. R. W. Southern calls the period of ca. 1050–1300 "the age of growth."[6] The monasteries had tilled the land, reaped its wealth, and put the profits into the improvement of the land. The Crusades to recapture the Holy Land from the Moslems, while of questionable religious motivation, were an expression of maturing Western society flexing its muscles. They opened up trade with the Arabic world—increasing both Western Europeans' prosperity and their awareness of Middle Eastern life and culture. A prosperous and intellectually aroused society could well afford to build great churches and universities, endow the arts, and cultivate scholarship. Nathan Mitchell has remarked on the coincidence of the simultaneous emergence of the natural sciences and the forms of eucharistic devotion outside of the Mass (that is, elevations, visits to the sacrament, processions with the sacrament, and solemn benediction of the blessed sacrament);[7] both are a consequence of the innate empiricism of Western people and the world view that what is real is what is seen.

Unrest is often a byproduct of prosperity, and that characterizes the period ca. 1300–1550. Increasing commerce resulted in the growth of towns, and the allure of the city contributed to the decay of the feudal system. At the same time the rulers of emerging nation-states contended with the papacy for political power. Economic well-being contributed to the decadence of the monasteries, the ecclesiastical hierarchy, and the liturgy. The sumptuous provision of chantries to sing solemn liturgies meant that the choir usurped more and more of the people's role. At the same time people could afford to pay stipends for the celebration of votive masses, and this increased the sheer number of private masses being celebrated and the number of mass-priests needed to celebrate them. Both developments contributed greatly to the disintegration of the communal nature of the liturgy. The people were thus being alienated from corporate worship precisely at the time when they needed its sustenance to deal with drastically changing social and political conditions. It is no wonder that they turned to paraliturgical devotions such as the rosary or the way of the cross, where their participation was assured, or to forms of contemplation and meditation. The *devotio moderna* of the fourteenth and fifteenth centuries encouraged a spirituality that was characteristically introspective and personal.[8]

Heirs of the Reformation often speak with pride of the "purification" of liturgy in the sixteenth century—for example, stripping away unscriptural accretions, putting worship back into the vernacular language, encouraging popular participation through congregational singing, and the like.[9] Yet a case can be made that this too was a product of sociocultural influence. There had been notable attempts at liturgical reform in the fifteenth century by such renewalists as Cardinal Nicholas of Cusa.[10] Renaissance humanism could not tolerate superstitious piety and cluttered rites. It should be noted that humanist reformers like Martin Bucer and Ulrich Zwingli carried out more thoroughgoing revisions of the liturgy than did Martin Luther, who was greatly steeped in the piety of the late Middle Ages (as witness his reluctance to give up the elevation of the host and cup in the Mass). The humanist concern was to make worship intelligible. The telltale sign of reformed liturgies are didactic exhortations to the people and preambles to the rites. The desire to reduce everything to an obvious meaning resulted in squeezing out the element of mystery. Reformation liturgies can be viewed as the attempt to limit everything in worship to the communication of meaning. Ritual action gave way to verbal pedagogy. This process even had some implications for church architecture. In Lutheran churches the pulpit was brought closer to the altar. In Reformed churches the pulpit dominated the altar so totally that in time the altar disappeared and was replaced by a table used for Holy Communion only a few times a year.[11] The preaching of the Word dominated the service. This has been taken as the consequence of the so-called rediscovery of the Bible. But the rediscovery of the Bible was also the consequence of the invention of the printing press, a cultural phenomenon which, as we shall see, Marshall McLuhan makes much of.

A political consequence of the Reformation was the increase of territorial political authority and political absolutism. The post-Reformation period in liturgy is marked by a desire for uniformity of usage. This is manifested in the Act of Uniformity of 1559 in which the English Parliament legislated the exclusive use of the *Book of Common Prayer* throughout the realm; in the establishment of a Congregation of Rites by the Council of Trent, whose function was to pronounce judgment on what was liturgically lawful; and in the strict enforcement of the church orders *(Kirchenordnungen)* in Lutheran territories. As an example that liturgical practice cannot be imposed by fiat, we would note the emergence in each of these traditions of groups which reacted against bureaucratic enforcement: Puritanism, Gallicanism, and Pietism. Each of these groups challenged ecclesiastical authority and unwittingly contributed to the wholesale challenge of theological and political authority in the Age of Rationalism.

All the Western churches in the eighteenth century were influenced by Rationalism, although the Enlightenment was strongest in Germany and affected Lutheran and Reformed liturgy more than Catholic or Anglican liturgy. A certain liturgical deteriorization had already occurred under Pietism, where the fixed and recurring liturgical elements were often made to yield to more subjective and extemporaneous ones. But under Rationalism the historic liturgy disappeared altogether. The Age of Reason valued religion according to its ethical results. Consequently, the church became a lecture hall and the minister a moral instructor. He felt free to rearrange the service at will, even to devise updated texts of the Lord's Prayer and the words of institution and distribution at Holy Communion. The following are some examples:[12]

Most High Father; let it be our supreme purpose to glorify Thee; let truth thrive among us; let virtue already dwell here as it does in heaven; reward our industry with bread, and our forgiving disposition with grace; from severe conflicts preserve us; and finally let all evil cease; that Thou art powerful, wise, and good over all—let this forever be our confidence.

Eat this bread; may the spirit of devotion rest upon you with all its blessings.
Drink a little wine; moral power does not reside in this wine, but in you, in the teachings of God, and in God.

Or:

Use this bread in remembrance of Jesus Christ; he that hungreth after pure and noble virtue shall be filled.
Drink a little wine; he that thirsteth after pure and noble virtue shall not long for it in vain.

Church music in the eighteenth century followed suit as musicians imported into church services the sentimental style of the Italian operatic aria. Plainsong chant, the chorale, and the polyphonic motet fell out of use. The factors that contaminated church music nourished the blooming concert and theater music of the eighteenth century. This, in turn, attracted the best musicians of the age, which led to the dissolution of the institutional foundations of Protestant church music in Germany. Amateur choirs replaced the school choirs. After the death of J. S. Bach, the best composers found employment outside the church, a situation which had an unfortunate affect on church music. The musical vocabulary which was so richly expanded by Mozart, Haydn, Beethoven, Schubert, Chopin, Berlioz, Wagner, and Brahms could also be used with much less telling effect by amateurs and hacks. Techniques that could engender gripping emotion could also engender trite sentimentality, as is amply demonstrated by nineteenth century hymns and anthems.[13]

The relative calm of the Age of Reason was shattered by the turbulence of the French Revolution, the Napoleonic Wars, and the Industrial Revolution. The early Romantics were preoccupied with the fact and idea of revolution. The various revolutions seemed to promise that, by breaking free from outmoded concepts and institutions, humanity might also escape suffering and oppression. These hopes did not materialize as expected, and as time went on a number of sensitive spirits felt an anxious sense of something lost. Mature Romanticism was not so much an attitude of freedom from the past as a quest for the recovery, indeed, a repristination, of an idealized past. The nineteenth century was a great age for the revival of folk culture and the fairy tale (for example, the Grimm brothers and Hans Christian Anderson), chivalry and the quest for the Holy Grail (for example, Tennyson's *Morte d'Arthur* and Wagner's *Parsifal*), and the resurgence of Gothic architecture (for example, Ruskin's *The Stones of Venice*). One looks for a golden age in which to take refuge from times of uncertainty. The Oxford Movement in England with its interest in High Church sacramentology and ritualism paralleled the Romantic movements in art and literature. The Confessional Revival Movement in Germany had as a part of its program the restoration of sixteenth-century liturgical orders, hymnody, and chant. The Ultramontane Movement in Roman Catholicism idealized the medieval church order and theology, and the Slavophile Movement in Russian Orthodoxy idealized the Greek fathers and the Slavic tradition.

It is noteworthy that the modern liturgical movement was born during the Age of Romanticism. The start of the movement is usually traced to the work of Dom Prosper Guéranger and the beginning of his monumental work *L'Anée liturgique* in 1840.[14] Guéranger was especially interested in the revival of the divine office and Gregorian chant in the renewed Benedictine abbeys of the nineteenth century. The great interest in the historical study of the liturgy in the nineteenth century laid the groundwork for the more pastoral phase of the liturgical movement in the twentieth century. The movement can be viewed in part as a critique of modern Western individualism as fostered by the industrial and technological revolutions. Against this it held up the image of the church as the mystical body of Christ and sought to return to the theological and ecclesiological concepts of the patristic period. This can be viewed as a romantic quest for a golden age. At the same time, however, patristic-inspired reflection, such as the "mystery theology" of Dom Odo Casel in the 1920s, opened the door to phenomenological studies by Christian liturgists; phenomenology underscored the concept of *leitourgia* as "the work of the people"; the emphasis on the corporate nature of worship led to agitation for the vernacular in order to encourage popular participation; and vernacularization required an openness to contemporary art, music, literature, and architecture. In a rather interesting way, what began as a kind of archaeological reconstruction became the foundation for a very contemporary edifice.

The Christian Cult in American Culture

A distinctive culture has emerged in America which has influenced the Free Church traditions more than the liturgical churches, although the latter have not totally escaped "Americanization." The Methodist liturgist James F. White has highlighted four liturgical eras in America during the last one hundred years that are largely a reflection of the cultural and social situation. They are revivalism, respectability, the recovery of tradition, and pluralism.[15]

Revivalism reflected the dominant cultural ethos of nineteenth-century America: pragmatic optimism. America was liberated from the past; the future was open and dazzling (one only need think of Manifest Destiny, the frontier spirit, and Horatio Alger). If one used the right techniques, there was no end to what one could accomplish. Revivalism viewed worship in much the same way: the techniques of preaching, prayer, and singing could be used to make converts. If the theology of revivalism was weak (for example, dividing all humanity into the saved and the damned), its pragmatism was strong. It had a rather accurate understanding of human behavior and knew how to manipulate it.

The problem for revivalism was that the same fervor could not be passed on to the next generation; so it was followed by a period of religious respectability. Respectability came to Protestant worship in the 1920s and 1930s. Emphases during this era included sobriety over the ecstatic, refinement over the primitive, restraint over the boisterous, and intelligibility over the emotional. Here again there was a reciprocity between cult and culture. Americans were becoming more sophisticated as education became available to greater numbers. "Enriching our worship" became the slogan of the era. The aesthetic experience replaced the conversion experience. Neo-Gothic buildings replaced the white frame meetinghouses. Full choirs singing "good" music replaced the gospel quartet, even if the choirs were not always up to performing the music they attempted to sing. Naturally, both choirs and clergy had to be suitably vested in their fine new buildings.

The emphasis shifted after World War II. The experience of the war crushed the shallow theology of the social gospel. Neo-orthodox theology emphasized the sinfulness of humanity and had a correspondingly high Christology. Wilsonian optimism gave way to the calculations of the cold war. We lived under the shadow of the bomb in the age of anxiety. In this situation, people looked for the security of identity and found it in a recovery of tradition. The historic rites were appreciated now for theological rather than aesthetic reasons. The names that stand out in this liturgical period are the great historians who probed the development of the liturgy: Josef Jungmann (Roman Catholic), Gregory Dix (Anglican), Luther D. Reed (Lutheran), William D. Maxwell (Presbyterian), and J. E. Rattenbury (Methodist).

Just when it seemed that a heritage was being recovered, American society came unglued in the 1960s. By 1970 it was hard to achieve consensus on anything (hair style, clothing, morality, life style, and the like). We discovered gaps between the generations, the races, economic classes, and the government and the governed. In such a situation of cultural pluralism, it was inevitable that we would take a more pluralistic approach toward worship. Experimentation became the order of the day. This is reflected in the various denominational liturgical committees called into being during the 1960s (for example, the Standing Liturgical Commission of the Episcopal Church, the Inter-Lutheran Commission on Worship, the Commission on Worship of the Methodist Church). Faced with a pluralistic society, these committees all decided to proceed with provisional material until some kind of consensus emerged which would make it possible to produce a definitive worship book. This has been called an era of "paperback liturgies."

At the same time, we should recognize that the main impetus for liturgical revision in these various church bodies came from the Second Vatican Council, which prepared the *Constitution on the Sacred Liturgy* in 1963. The immense scholarly and pastoral work of the modern liturgical movement lies behind this document which set the agenda for Roman Catholic liturgical change. Catholic liturgical revision has been very influential on Protestant liturgical work. The Catholic three-year Sunday and festival lectionary was probably Catholicism's greatest gift to Protestant biblical preaching. The International Consultation on English Texts (ICET) was established in 1969 to translate into English common liturgical texts used by Christians of many denominations who worship in English. These appeared as *Prayers We Have in Common* (1970; revised 1976). It was a period of great ecumenical borrowing.

Now, it seems, the age of experimentation is largely over. Definitive new worship resources have been published, including the Roman Missal, Lectionary, and Sacramentary in the early 1970s, the Presbyterian Worshipbook in 1972, the new *Book of Common Prayer* of the Episcopal Church in 1977 (officially adopted in 1979), and the *Lutheran Book of Worship* in 1978. The United Methodists are at work producing a major new worship resource which will share many of the same characteristics as these others. But as James White suggests, experimentation affected our worship in some irrevocable ways. We were forced to become more inclusive in our thinking, more imaginative in our planning, more ritually resourceful in our leadership, more ecumenically aware in our use of resources, and more socially responsible in our praying and preaching.[16]

As we implement these new worship resources in our parishes, we should be aware of areas where our culture influences our cultic practices. Kenneth Smits has defined American Catholic liturgical reform as profoundly marked by (1) consumerism; (2) individuality, creativity, and spontaneity; (3) voluntarism; (4) pragmatism; and (5) amateurism.[17] These same characteristics of American culture have affected Protestant liturgical renewal. If free enterprise and competition has flooded the market with bulletins, inserts, homily helps, and other liturgical consumer items, it has also diminished creative efforts on the part of parish worship planners. If mass communication and high mobility have created a high level of tolerance for liturgical change, it has also dulled the appetite for solid and steady spiritual fare. If the shopping around for a liturgy that suits one's taste, which characterizes many churchgoers today, has aroused, as a positive consequence, a concern on the part of pastors and lay leaders to upgrade the quality of what is done in worship, it also bespeaks the privatization of faith that makes the formation of a viable worshiping community all but impossible. If concern to attract and keep worshipers has led us to plan liturgies that are conveniently timed and easily assimilable, it has also allowed us to escape the arduous task of serious reflection on our liturgical practices. We are far too easily pleased with what works, even if what works undermines the integrity of the church and its public work. If we have gotten everyone into the liturgical act by our emphasis on lay participation, we have also usually failed to provide the training necessary to enable worship leaders to carry out their roles with knowledge, sensitivity, and enduring results.

This brief analysis of the blessing and bane of celebrating liturgy in our culture should alert us to the twin dangers of what Smits calls "cultural capitulation" and "cultural irrelevancy." We cannot avoid bringing our culture to church with us; it is a part of our very being. But in the light of tradition we need to sort out those cultural influences that contribute to the integrity of Christian worship from those that detract from it. We will especially want to exploit those aspects of our culture which reinforce what Christian worship and the church should be at their best. Certainly one aspect of American culture which is worth exploring is *cultural pluralism*. In the array of ethnic customs and experiences which make up American society we have the possibility of experiencing the catholicity or wholeness of the church, especially in congregations which intentionally reach out to embrace all sorts of people in their fellowship. Because cross-cultural experience is one way to transcend the limitations of particular cultures while recognizing the value of culture, it seems appropriate to conclude this chapter with some brief reflections on what American black and Hispanic cultures may contribute to Christian worship generally.

It would, of course, be a mistake to look upon the black or Hispanic cultures as monolithic. There has always been a sector of the black population which has identified more with white society than with black, in religious expression as well as in other matters.[18] While more than half of churchgoing Blacks are members of Baptist churches, there has also been a sizable group of black Catholics. Among Hispanics one may distinguish between those of West Indian and those of Mexican extraction. While the overwhelming majority of Hispanics are Roman Catholic, there is a rapidly growing number of Hispanic pentecostals. Small percentages of both Blacks and Hispanics belong to mainline Protestant churches. Neither the Black nor the Hispanic religious experience can be stereotyped, but it may still be asserted that the most important cultic contributions of American Blacks and Hispanics, respectively, are music in worship[19] and the sense of *fiesta*.[20]

The emotionalism that is identified with black worship is most evident in the musical quality of black worship and the music itself. Plain talking, praying, and proclaiming the gospel can turn into chantlike singing, indicative of the fact that worship is an ecstatic event in which we praise God with our whole being and not just with our minds. The music in black worship runs the gamut from classical hymns and anthems to jazzy, improvised gospel songs. In between are the revival hymns learned from white evangelical missionaries, hymns composed by black clergy and laypersons (for example, "I'll Live On," "Stand By Me," "Precious Lord, Take My Hand," and "Lift Every Voice and Sing"), and the spirituals which originated in the experience of slavery.[21] The spirituals have an especially appropriate liturgical character because they stress biblical and/or theological themes and (like Gregorian chant) represent the anonymous contribution of a worshiping community rather than the individual expression of a particular poet or composer. The overall range of the music used in black worship represents a versatility of which few white congregations could boast.

If black persons found release from suffering in singing and shouting, Hispanics transcended misery by celebrating life with a *fiesta*. Vigilio Elizondo has written that "the Latino does not party because things are going well, or because there are no problems or difficulties; he celebrates because he is alive. He celebrates because of his sense of the tragic, accepting the many different forces of life and yet realizing there is the ultimate happiness which has already begun."[22] *Fiesta* injects a sense of eschatological fulfillment in the midst of the tribulations of this world.

The Hispanic is a hybrid mixture of the Spanish and the American Indian. From Spain he inherited a Christian tradition with roots in Asia Minor which took a decidedly mystical turn during many centuries of Moorish domination. From the American Indian he acquired a closeness to nature and a sense of wonder which is the precondition for any genuine worship. As Ricardo Ramirez has written, "All of these elements have contributed to an aura of mysticism, fantasy and wonder in the religion of Mexico, of the Mexican American and other Hispanic peoples in the United States. This peculiar and complex religious sense merits serious study so that liturgists may understand what it is in fiesta, carnival, theatre, magic, symbolism and tradition which appeals to Hispanic cultures";[23] indeed, so that we may better understand the basic appeal of festival and celebration for all people.

4

the language of WORSHIP

The Effectiveness of Liturgical Media

If cult as well as culture requires the transmission of a body of belief and learned behavior from one generation to another, the issue of language looms in importance. Communication is what we understand language to be. Paul Hoon points out that communication in worship operates in at least five directions at once:[1]

1. from God to the gathered people;
2. from the gathered people to God;
3. by the gathered people to one another;
4. by the congregation to those outside the gathered community;
5. by those outside the gathered community to those within.

These directions of communication suggest the multiple problems of liturgical language. The least problematic is in terms of what the people say to God. This is why the language of prayer seems to change the least over the years, and people often prefer the words they learned in their youth—even if those words are in a different linguistic currency than what is normal for the present. In any case God's Word must get through to worshipers in terms which are meaningful or relevant to their lives.

Sometimes proclamation involves translation in order to bridge the chasm of history. That is one of the tasks of preaching. As Daniel Stevick points out, some words get worn out or stale through overuse; other words change their meaning during the course of history.[2] Nevertheless, translation does not necessarily require a new vocabulary. It is possible to learn a special vocabulary within the life of a community of faith. The real problem of vocabulary comes when the community reaches out to embrace others. Then the kind of terminology which might be acceptable in the liturgical context is less than functionally effective when it is used in the service of evangelization. This recognition suggests that the ancient distinction between the liturgy of the catechumens and the liturgy of the faithful might acquire a contemporary relevance. The kind of worship to which outsiders are drawn is not necessarily the kind of worship which will meet the needs of insiders. The kind of preaching one does with catechumens is not the kind of preaching one regularly inflicts on the faithful. Catechumenal worship will be heavily didactic (for example, note the worship style used for Sunday or vacation church schools); the worship of the faithful tends to be more celebrational and devotional.

The dialogue between insiders and outsiders raises afresh the problem of vernacularization. This is a dialogue which also goes on within the fellowship of the church. Whatever gaps might be experienced between cult and culture are experienced within the cult as well as outside of it. This exacerbates the problem of finding a common liturgical vocabulary because church members are not all at the same place on the continuum of the range of relationships between cult and culture. Thus, some worshipers prefer a secularized liturgical language and others prefer a sacralized form of expression. Because tradition itself is a form of sacralization, one solution to this problem has been to retain the bipolar tension between traditional and contemporary speech. Thus, the Episcopal *Book of Common Prayer* provides both traditional and contemporary texts of the eucharistic rite, prayer offices, and the collects. However, the *Lutheran Book of Worship* is even more rigorous in its use of contemporary speech, although we would note that the 1789 Prayer Book text of the Lord's Prayer is consistently printed side by side with the 1975 International Consultation on English Texts (ICET) translation of the Lord's Prayer. This would appear consistent with the common Lutheran practice of bilingual, Latin-vernacular liturgies in the sixteenth and seventeenth centuries.

The use of non-sexist language in the *Lutheran Book of Worship* must also be applauded as a way of raising the consciousness of the believer concerning the eschatological nature of the church in which there is no distinction between men and women, social classes, and races (Gal. 3:28). On the other hand, nonsexist language risks depriving God of his personal character. Therefore, the task which is still before us is really to find ways of expanding our vision of God by employing feminine imagery of God alongside masculine imagery. Biblical exegetes have noted some feminine characteristics of Jesus as well as masculine characteristics. Some contemporary theologians have pointed out how a renewal of the doctrine of the Holy Spirit can contribute to finding feminine images of God since the Spirit suggests a feminine sense of accessibility, nurture, and love.

The matter of vocabulary does not exhaust the problem of liturgical language. Language is communication in all its dimensions. We need to see that everything in worship communicates, for example, the physical bearing of the worship leaders, choir, and acolytes, the liturgical tempo, the symbols on the altar, the kind of bread and wine used for Holy Communion, the clergy's vestments, the location of the font, the illumination of the windows, the architectural style, the carpeting, and so on. The white frame New England meetinghouse communicates something different theologically as well as aesthetically from the medieval Gothic cathedral. The order of service is a powerful form of communication (including the style of type in which it is printed). In summation, all aspects of worship communicate and may therefore be considered language of worship.

It is precisely because all these facets of worship communicate that they have never been quite the adiaphora, or indifferent matters, that Lutheran theology made them out to be. The same theologians who would call the forms of worship adiaphora would also fight vicious battles over the elevation of the host and chalice, the symbolic breaking of bread, the baptismal exorcism, and so forth. No symbol is empty, but they may not always appeal to our reason. In fact, they are quite often *felt* in evocative ways to express meanings which appeal to the senses, the emotions, or the aesthetic sense. Even sermons appeal more often to our feelings than to our reason. We are more often struck by the way in which a sermon is delivered than by what is said. In the famous phrase of Marshall McLuhan, "The medium is the message."

McLuhan distinguished between hot and cool media. A medium is hot or cool depending on the extent to which the information given has to be filled in or completed by the recipient. Thus, McLuhan suggests that "Telephone is a cool medium . . . because the ear is given a meagre amount of information. And speech is a cool medium . . . because so little is given and so much has to be filled in by the listener. On the other hand, hot media do not have so much to be filled in or completed by the audience. Hot media are, therefore, low in participation or completion by the audience."[3] To take two other celebrated examples, reading is a hot medium because the information is organized for us on the printed page. Television is a cool medium because our eyes have to organize the dots and lines on the screen into an image. The information on the screen is organized by our bodies.

Those who have grown up with electric media are used to having their senses massaged or revitalized. Our culture itself has become highly sensate. Attendant to this has been a lower ability to concentrate on one medium for an extended period of time, especially a hot one. This has upset parents and teachers who are straying travelers from the age of Gutenberg and the printing press. Colleges and universities find that students have difficulty concentrating on lectures and heavy reading, so they are moving toward learning models which require "participation or completion by the audience," that is, models in which the student must internally organize and appropriate the data.

This has serious implications for the language of worship. It suggests that worship will communicate better in our culture if it is a multimedia event which stimulates a number of senses at once. In McLuhan's terms, worship needs to be a cool medium rather than a hot one. It must require a higher level of participation in the sense of "completion by the audience" than much of mainline Protestant and post-Vatican II Roman Catholic worship has provided. Since the Renaissance, the whole Western church has suffered from the mistaken notion that a religion is true to the extent to which it is immediately and entirely intelligible. As a consequence worship has become more and more didactic. Protestant liturgies have been burdened with lengthy introductions to ritual acts and exhortations to the participants. Roman Catholic missals used to include commentaries on the Mass as well as a translation of the text. After Vatican II the commentaries were given orally by a narrator, a practice that is hopefully waning. However necessary all this instruction may have been in the sixteenth century as a corrective of late medieval superstition, we must agree with Louis Bouyer that "at the present stage of human evolution we are suffering from the tyranny of the word, or rather of words that have been devitalized by the very stress that has been placed upon them."[4]

A corollary of "the tyranny of the word" is the tyranny of the service book. With the invention of printing in the fifteenth century came liturgical standardization. Variation, either intentional or unintentional, was always possible with handwritten missals and breviaries in the Middle Ages. Every ecclesiastical province and religious order had its own liturgical books. The preface to the 1549 *Book of Common Prayer* mentions five different provincial liturgical uses in England and then decreed that "Now from hencefurth, all the whole realme shall haue but one use."[5] What was begun by the Protestants was picked up by the Catholics. In reaction to the various Protestant rites, the Council of Trent decreed in 1563 that all churches under the papacy should follow the Roman rite unless their own local usage was more than two hundred years old. The council fathers also entrusted the curia with the task of producing a standard missal and breviary, which appeared swiftly during the pontificate of Pius V as the *Breviarium Romanum* (1568) and the *Missale Romanum* (1570).[6]

Given the pressure toward liturgical uniformity in the sixteenth century, Martin Luther represented an old-fashioned point of view. As he wrote *Against the Heavenly Prophets* in 1524, "I am happy the mass is now held among the Germans in German. But to make a necessity of this, as if it had to be so, is again too much. This spirit cannot do anything else than continually create laws, necessity, problems of conscience, and sin."[7] He felt that each local or territorial church ought to be free to develop its own forms of worship, even to retain Latin texts where there were choirs capable of singing the Gregorian chants he admired so much. As a result, some one hundred thirty-five Lutheran church orders appeared in Germany alone between 1523 and 1555.[8] Thereafter an increasing standardization of liturgical use became evident, especially in the period of orthodoxy.

Standardization was made possible by the mass printing of books. It fostered the attitude that a new service book renders the previous ones obsolete. It makes difficult the task of adapting or indigenizing the liturgy in new cultural situations since the missionaries bring their books with them. (This problem applies to home missions as well as foreign missions.) It militates against the development of a variety of liturgical roles since the clergy and laity generally shared the same book. The publication of a ministers edition as well as a pew edition of the *Lutheran Book of Worship* in 1978 represents the breakthrough of an older and better idea.

In the early Middle Ages several books were needed for the celebration of the Eucharist. An *ordo* provided the order of service and the rubrics governing the celebration. The celebrant needed a sacramentary, which contained the prayers of the Mass; the subdeacon needed an *apostolus* or epistolary in order to read the epistles; the deacon needed an *evangelarium* or gospelary in order to read the Gospels; the choir needed an antiphonary for the proper chants (Introit, Gradual, Offertory, and Holy Communion) and a *liber usualis* for the ordinary chants (Kyrie, Gloria, Credo, Sanctus, and Agnus Dei). This plethora of books may seem to have made worship very complicated, and it did; but it also ensured various liturgical roles. The missal was invented in the thirteenth century to meet the needs of friars who had to be on the road by assembling all the texts necessary for the Mass into one handy book. This may have simplified things, but it also contributed to the diminishing of the corporate spirit of worship. It made the private mass possible.[9] It also limited the number of options. Jungmann points out that the most ancient of the Roman mass books, the Verona Sacramentary (the so-called "Leonine"), has a proper preface for each mass: "thus, although it is quite incomplete, the sacramentary has 267 prefaces! Even the older *Gelasianum* still furnishes 54 prefaces, the later *Gelasianum* in the St. Gall manuscript, 186."[10] While this number was drastically reduced in the Gregorian Sacramentary, the Middle Ages was not happy with such poverty. So various missals introduced new prefaces. The missal of 1570 reduced the number to eleven!

Naturally, worshipers complain when they must maneuver their way through the liturgy, juggling books and assorted sheets of paper, trying desperately to follow the presiding minister as he hops from one option to another. The answer to such a problem is not to reduce the number of options; it is to free people from the tyranny of printed material. A whole repertoire of responses can easily be learned from memory, especially with the help of music. Over a period of time the congregation's need to use the worship book can be reduced to hymns and psalms. The eye can be freed from the page so that the worshiper may look at other things in the liturgical environment while the ear fastens on the words (which means that texts must be spoken or sung audibly and distinctly).

Liberating worshipers from the service book might produce a rippling effect with other liberating consequences. The book is often something the body can hide behind. If the barrier is gone the worshiper might feel free to inject his body more actively into worship.

He might begin to sway or tap his foot and reach out to greet his neighbors during the greeting of peace and move less self-consciously to Holy Communion. He may begin to resist such artificial intrusions as a fussy ushering of people to the communion rail or out of church at the end of the service. "Formal" worship in the sense of following a particular form does not mean that the character of worship should be formal in the social-psychological sense.

If the worshiper is going to be encouraged to use a number of senses simultaneously, there are times when his attention must be summoned to something in particular. In the otherwise multimedia Eastern Orthodox worship, the deacon summons the concentration of the worshiper before something important such as the Scripture readings by saying, "Let us be attentive." This is a rather simple but direct device. Something of the same order can be accomplished more subtly if the worship leaders keep the service moving in a straightforward direction. It has been said that the attention of the worshiper is grasped or lost within the first five minutes. Perhaps it was for this reason that various recent revisions of the eucharistic liturgy sought to unclutter the entrance rite. Following the precedent set by the new Roman Mass, the rubrics in the new *Book of Common Prayer* and the *Lutheran Book of Worship* recommend that either the Kyrie or the Song of Praise be sung, but both only on great festivals. Those festivals might also be the occasions when the confession of sins preceding the service is omitted.[11] The entrance rite should not call attention to itself. It should lead the worshipers with dispatch to the first major liturgical act: the proclamation of the Word of God, which is introduced by the prayer of the day. Nor should it slow down the pace of the liturgy because it contains too much. It should be proportionate to the function of assembling the people and the ministers and appropriate to the nature of the occasion, the time, and the place.

Tempo is an important factor in listening to prayers or Scripture readings. The worshiper must simultaneously hear the words, comprehend their meaning, and (in the case of prayer) make them his own address to God or (in the case of Scripture) apply the text to his own situation. This argues for a slow reading pace, but not too slow lest boredom set in. It also argues for declamation which manages to steer between the "dramatic heavy" and the "stained-glass voice," lest meaning be prematurely (and perhaps erroneously) inflicted on the text, or there be no meaning at all.

Proportion is another ingredient in effective communication through liturgical media. This might mean many things, such as preserving the right amount of balance between sameness and variety in the elements of the service; estimating how much verbal, musical, visual, or olfactory stimulation a congregation can receive and still find the worship experience meaningful; determining what emphasis to give to each part of the service; or finding ways of blending into a unified experience the intelligible and the mysterious, the sense of immanence and the sense of transcendence.

The right tempo and proportion of a service will contribute to the *vitality* of worship. Christian liturgy is, indeed, a celebration of the redeemed life, the eschatological life of the kingdom of God which is fitfully lived in the midst of the old life of sin and death. In fact, Christian worship is always carried out under the sign of the cross, a symbol intruding on this celebration of new life. But in the words of that ancient antiphon from the veneration of the cross in the Good Friday liturgy, "through the cross joy has come to the whole world." Indeed, joy through the cross should provide the tone of Christian worship.

Vitality requires that liturgical language be in the active tense and indicative mood, that it be characterized by movement and action. This does not mean that the liturgy should be loaded down with ceremonies and gestures—again, one must maintain a sense of proportion—but rather that liturgy should get us to where it is going in an unencumbered way. Ceremonies and gestures should serve to propel it along, not to confuse the direction. The communion service is a good example of a rite where the actions can lead us in a straight-forward way to the desired conclusion. This service moves with a direct, dramatic force, unimpeded by excessive devotional comment and musical interlude as we do what Jesus did when he took the bread and cup, gave thanks over them, broke the bread, and dis-tributed these to his disciples. Christians have always wanted to linger over these actions and add devotional reflection to each move-ment. This is how the offertory prayers, the Lord's Prayer, the fraction prayers, and the communion prayers found entree into the order of service. Originally the eucharistic prayer said all that needed to be said. There has also been a desire to linger in meditation after the distribution of Holy Communion. Hence the inclusion of postcommunion canticles such as the *Nunc dimittis* and postcommunion prayers. These elements were laid over the more primitive abrupt dismissal of the communicants, unprotracted by music or further speech. Liturgical revision in both Roman Catholic and Protestant churches has moved in the direction of pruning the liturgy of some of its more luxurious growth in order to let the simple shape stand clear. The need for devotion has been provided by the inclusion of periods of silent reflection rather than more orations, for the proportion of silence to speech and the proper pacing of silence as well as speech will also contribute to liturgical vitality.

The Role of Art in Worship

Vocabulary, tempo, proportion, and vitality are, of course, concerns of art as well as liturgy. It is clear that all the arts have a contribution to make to Christian worship. The people assemble in a building to do their liturgy. They hear and speak words which must endure for longer than a week at a time. Some of these words are set to music either because they are ecstatic speech or because the tunes help people to learn and remember them. Vessels, books, and vestments are used and, minimally, there is the need for a table. A settled congregation, like a settled family, will tend to collect other pieces of furniture and memorabilia. There is, therefore, architecture, poetry, music, design, and plastic art employed in worship.

All the arts can make a contribution to Christian worship. But this is not the same as saying that liturgy is an art form. Worship is more than an aesthetic experience. The fact that art and liturgy have similar ways of communicating should not lead us to think that they communicate the same vision. They are distinct visions of reality. Art has its own message to proclaim, its own claims to make, sometimes its own cultus to develop.

The Christian tradition has rightfully been wary of art and artists even when it employs them in its service. Paul Hoon warns against "the corruption of aestheticism," which he describes as:

> . . . the autonomy with which art insinuates its vision of reality into liturgy and takes captive the Christian substance of liturgy; the conscious or unconscious affirmation art commonly makes that the reality

which Christianity names 'God' is most authentically experienced as Beauty rather than as the Holy; the understanding of the action of liturgy as involving man's imagination and feeling more than his conscience and will; the conviction—admitted or unadmitted—which art often communicates that the essence of the experience of worship is pleasure and the consequent acceptance of artistic canons is decisive for the substance and form of worship.[12]

Hoon is not unappreciative of the immense contributions of the arts to the revitalization of the language of worship. But the demise of Puritan restraints in the Free Church tradition, signaled by the employment of the hitherto anathematized organs in the mid-nineteenth century in the absence of stable liturgical forms, has left the door wide open to the corruptions Hoon warns of. But it is not only a Free Church problem. The aestheticism of the Enlightenment has insinuated itself into all the traditions of Western Christianity.

Johann Sebastian Bach may have been one of the last of the giants of art in Western culture to understand his role in the church as diaconal. Certainly Bach was open to the musical currents of the early eighteenth century. But on the basis of the considerable research into the question of Bach's relationship to the Enlightenment, Jaroslav Pelikan concludes that the cantor of St. Thomas Church in Leipzig "was vastly out of sympathy with the religiosity of the Enlightenment and with the theology which that religiosity produced."[13] This could not help but affect Bach's aesthetic principles as far as music for the church was concerned. Not only were his texts the Holy Scriptures and hymn verses which had an enduring place in Christian worship, but so were his tunes. Most of the church cantatas are based on the great chorales which were sung in the Lutheran churches in the sixteenth and seventeenth centuries. Most of these chorales even had a liturgical assignment (for example, *Wachet Auf* was sung on the last Sunday of the church year). What Bach did with these chorales demonstrates an astute openness to contemporary musical vocabulary, but it is an adaptation of tradition rather than an abandonment of it. He built on the work of his predecessors, from Michael Praetorius to Scheidt, Schein, Schütz, Buxtehude, Pachelbel, Weckmann, and others. It was because his music was traditional that Bach was abandoned after his death. When his music was revived a hundred years later, it was not because it was so churchly but because it was great music. Nevertheless, it would be profitable to study Bach's church music from a theological as well as from a musical perspective.

The liturgical artist, like Bach, is primarily a servant of the Word celebrated in the worshiping community. Liturgical art is bound to the liturgical forms within which it works, even though it might enrich those forms. However, the kind of subjectivism and individualism that some artists have cultivated since the Enlightenment is out of place in the liturgy. By definition liturgical art must be communal. The diaconal role of the liturgical artist is expressed in the words of Joseph Gelineau: "In the celebration of Christian worship it is Christ who is expressing Himself in His visible Body, the Church. The message which art should transmit is not that of any individual man, no matter how great his genius or profound his mind. . . . The composer puts his art at the disposal of the community. . . . It is not his place, by claiming a sincerity which is but psychological, to provide the community with 'his' music, nor to propose 'his' sentiments, nor to impose 'his' idiom."[14] From within this role, however, a number of the insights of art can be brought to bear on the language of worship.

Art can teach us a great deal about *style.* Style is a distinctive way of doing or saying something. Style means consistency of expression. In other words, the language of worship should not contradict itself. Words, gestures, music, architecture, vestments, and paraments ought to cohere and contribute to a unified experience. There might be something incoherent, for example, about Elizabethan English set to jazz sung by choirboys in medieval choir vesture in a suburban church-in-the-round.

Consistency does not mean a bland sameness. It means establishing certain ways of doing things which take account of the size and character of the congregation, the nature of the liturgical space, the time of the service, the liturgical options available, and the integrity of the rite. For example, a communion service held on a weekday morning in a small chapel with a dozen worshipers present who are probably on their way to work will have a different style than the chief Sunday morning Eucharist. The service will probably be spoken rather than sung; a number of texts might be omitted (for example, the Kyrie, Song of Praise, one of the lessons and the psalmody, the creed, hymns, offertory, and postcommunion songs); the homily will be kept under five minutes; and the whole service will have more of an informal and spontaneous quality than the Sunday liturgy.

Another way of demonstrating a variety of usage within a consistency of style is in the choice of vestments for the presiding and assisting ministers. Thus, while the presider might wear a luxurious chasuble over alb and stole for the Sunday liturgy, a more simple chasuble or none at all might be worn at the weekday liturgy. The assistants might wear dalmatics over their albs at the Sunday liturgy, but only an alb or even street clothes at the weekday liturgy. At prayer offices the cassock and surplice might be retained for all ministers. The surplice, it should be remembered, is a variant of the alb having a larger neck opening and wider sleeves which made it quicker to don by clerics returning to the church from their other responsibilities in order to recite the canonical hours. Whether alb or surplice is worn at occasional services such as weddings and funerals might depend on whether they are celebrated in the context of the Eucharist. Finally, there is a venerable Protestant tradition of wearing black academic gowns (sometimes with tabs or *beffchen*) for preaching services. Vestments are a liturgical language. Do our choices contribute to a consistency of style while saying that different rites have a different character and history, or do they bespeak an undifferentiated sameness or even contribute to a confusion of liturgical experience? And what does the fabric and design of the vestments communicate: triumphalism or simplicity? Fullness or skimpiness? Gaudiness or dignity?

These questions are related to *taste,* which is a product of one's culture. Here we come to one of the most important contributions of art to the language of worship and one of the principal reasons the church has always felt inclined to let the artist in. Art is in touch with contemporary culture, either in a critical or in an affirmative way, but in touch nevertheless. If, as we said at the outset, the language of worship includes dialogue between those inside and outside the liturgical assembly, the sights and sounds of our "technopolitan" culture must find entree into our worship. Many of the faithful would be just as happy to keep the world out, but that would communicate something utterly foreign to the nature of the gospel which Christian liturgy celebrates. To be sure, Christian worship is an eschatological event. That should make it something different from the rest of life, but not in the sense of escaping from this world;

rather in the sense of transforming the life of the world—beholding it from the perspective of communion with the very God whom the rest of life may try to ignore. It is only from the perspective of the end of all things, proleptically realized in Christian worship, that "Earth and all stars! Loud rushing planets! Sing to the Lord a new song" (Herb Brokering, *Lutheran Book of Worship,* Hymn 558). Imploring the gift of faith, "the joyful sense of things unseen," we pray:

Beyond the lines of steel and stone,
Beneath the forms of flesh and bone,
Beyond the curve of time and space,
Show us the wonder of your face. (Royce Scherf, *Lutheran Book of Worship,* Hymn 201)

From such a vision we are impelled to reclaim even the ghastly light of the atoms for the light of Christ.

Great God, our source and Lord of space,
O Force of all by whose sheer pow'r
The primal fires that flared and raged
Were struck, blazed on, and still are made:
Oh, save us, Lord, at this fierce hour
From threat'ning fires that we have laid.

Great God of fire, incarnate flame,
Through Christ in whom your love has burned
And burns the way for our dark pace
On cosmic routes within us turned:
Lead us beyond atomic night;
Guide, Lord, in hope our broken race.

Lord of the atom, we praise your might,
Expressed in terrifying light;
Before us rise the flames as pyres,
Or bursts of love—they blind our sight.
Help us, our Lord, oh, help us see
New forms of peace through suff'ring fires. (George Utech, *Lutheran Book of Worship,* Hymn 466)

The language of science and technology finds its way into our hymnals. An occasional tone row ekes its way through a prelude performed on an electric appliance which inexpensively imitates the sounds of a pipe organ. Reinforced concrete and steel support the contoured structures of our church building. Simplicity of line and honesty of fabric characterize the new line of vestments and paraments marketed in this year's ecclesiastical arts catalogue. All this may be inspiring; it may also be banal. It may be critiqued or affirmed, but it cannot be ignored because we are still very much a part of the *saeculum*. We may welcome that or resent it, but if we are to communicate with our culture we must learn the language. In the words of Joseph Sittler, we must find "fresh forms of statement . . . to set forth ancient facts and encounters."[15] At the same time, fresh encounters may produce renewed appreciation of ancient statements. Both tradition and contemporaneity are served by a productive dialogue between cult and culture.

5

the action of WORSHIP

The Problem and Necessity of Ritual Action

It has been widely contended in recent years that modern Western people have lost an ability to communicate through ritual. It is asserted that many symbols that once had meaning for people no longer have meaning for some people today. The symbols no longer "speak," and therefore we have to speak for them. The liturgiologist, Romano Guardini, asked in 1964, "Would it not be better to admit that man in this industrial and scientific age, with its sociological structure, is no longer capable of the liturgical act?"[1]

The word "ritual" has negative connotations for many people. It is associated with "vain repetition," with cold formality, with going through the motions—in short, with insincerity. To be sure, those coming from traditions influenced by Puritanism or Pietism equate ritualistic religion with mindless repetition and mechanical worship. However anthropologist Mary Douglas observes that even many professional sociologists describe the ritualist as "one who performs external gestures without an inner commitment to the ideas being expressed."[2] Then what word do we use, she asks, to describe the person who performs external gestures and *is* inwardly committed to the ideas being expressed?

Our problem with repetition of ritual acts comes to focus when we Western Christians are confronted with the liturgical style of the Eastern churches. Our paradigm of liturgy is the classroom. We sit in straight rows facing in one direction and do what we are told. This is not so much community as collectivity. The concept of community is better expressed in the village character of the Eastern liturgy. Each person contributes at his or her own level to the total event. At times worshipers are doing their own thing (for example, lighting candles or kissing icons); at other times they come together for common things (for example, to hear the Gospel, to receive Holy Com-

68

munion). There is also a high degree of repetition in the prayer formularies that offends the orderly Western mind. "Again and again, in peace let us pray to the Lord. . . ."

Margaret Mead relates the story of an anthropology student who decided, as a course project, to make a study of the emotional impact of the ritual of the Roman Catholic High Mass. She was determined to be as objective and thorough as possible until the idea hit her that "they do this *every* Sunday." This shocking idea made it difficult for her to observe the rest of the ceremony. "Such an attitude," suggested Mead, "is widespread in America today; it is such an attitude toward the repetition of anything, ritual included, that undercuts our capacity to ritualize."[3]

We are also infected with the notion that the liturgy must have a certain rational progression. So we tend to force it in certain directions by means of commentaries and explanations—all of which tend to turn the liturgy into a rather dull and inefficient sermon and render the congregation correspondingly passive. Besides this, some of the explanations beg questions. For example, in what way is the recitation of the Creed *really* a response to the gospel? Liturgical action is symbolic action, and symbols are ambiguous and imprecise. They should be left this way so that they are capable of conveying an assortment of meanings. Well-done acts are also capable of conveying an assortment of meanings. A well-executed kiss can say "I love you" without the voicing of those words (although in our present state of ritual impoverishment we may need the words too!). In terms of liturgical action, however, my suspicion is that "bigger is better." Baptism by immersion and Eucharist with real bread and a common cup will do more to communicate the meaning of these sacraments than lengthy commentaries. As Josef Jungmann has reminded us, well-done liturgy is its own best catechesis. Our liturgical actions are in need of more urgent attention than our liturgical texts.

A related problem is our inability to celebrate a feast. We so overanticipate Christmas during the Advent season that we are exhausted and resourceless by December 25. So we close up our churches on Christmas Day in honor of Christ's birthday. We have yet to discover what Easter is all about, largely because we have divorced it from its baptismal context. The prospect of fifty days of continuous celebration of the Lord Jesus' resurrection just boggles the mind. In many congregations the great paschal feast comes grinding to a halt with the removal of the last lily from the altar on Easter Sunday. By Pentecost the members of the parish have taken off in their campers. All pastors know the problem of trying to get the people to church on festival days which lack widespread support from secular society. When some special commemoration does "take hold," Mead's observations about our peculiarly American problem with ritual repetition come into play—the people lose interest in it after a few years.

As evidence that the problem with ritual is largely an American cultural problem and not just a Christian or even a Protestant one, we cite a penetrating essay which appeared in *Time* magazine in October 1970.

> The gift of ritual is not exactly prospering in the 20th century; secularity, urbanism, technology—all contrive to separate modern man from the kind of community that encourages, even demands, a sense of ceremony. But is this the best that America can do for a bill of rites? Other people's rituals tend to release them—as they should. Rituals are society's unwritten permission for civilized man to express primitive emotions: fear, sexuality, grief. Other people's rituals invite them to be more human in public—more themselves—than they dare to be in private. Greek Zorbas whirl like fertility gods. Irishmen keen at their friends' funerals or even the funerals of strangers. Americans smile their Fixed Smile: the Smile as anti-smile—no pleasure, no love, no silliness. The Smile that tries to hide the face of American Gothic and only betrays it. The smile that says, "I cannot be myself in public."[4]

If this is the general cultural problem with ritual even in the non-religious sphere, it is a small wonder that we have problems ritualizing the cosmos-shaking events of Jesus' death and resurrection.

It is, of course, one thing to see the problem and something else to explain it so that we can try to overcome it. One of the few studies that gets at the roots of the move away from ritualism is Mary Douglas's *Natural Symbols*. She notes that ritual patterns vary from one experience to another because while "formal social relations call for controlled movements and physical distance, informal relations call for relaxed posture, free movement, casual dress, uninhibited speech, and so forth." Human relations are structured according to two independently varying criteria called "grid" and "group."[5] "Group" is the experience of a bounded social unit; "grid" refers to rules which relate one person to others on an ego-centered basis. Where group and grid are found together, relations tend to be well-ordered and clearly defined. Where group is strong, people tend to express themselves through the use of their bodies; that is, they relate more freely with one another. Where grid is strong, people have less commitment to the group and they are less cognizant of the body as a symbol of social relationships. The general lack of commitment to common symbols today suggests the lack of a strong grid, that is, accepted rules of social relationships.

Having established these definitions, Douglas proceeds to isolate three phases in the process of moving away from ritualism. "First, there is the *contempt* of external ritual forms; second, there is the private *internalizing* of religious experience; third, there is the move to humanist philanthropy. When the third stage is under way," she writes, "the symbolic life of the spirit is finished."[6] Ritual is most highly developed where symbolic action is held to be efficacious. Thus, a sacramental religion would be more attuned to ritual action than an ethical religion. This would not necessarily imply that a religion was at an "inferior" stage of development if it had a highly developed ritual system. Against Robertson Smith, it can no longer be held that all primitive religions are magical and taboo-ridden or that all "advanced" religions are ethically oriented. Colin M. Turnbull's study of the Pygmies of the Ituri Forest in Africa shows that the Pygmies are bound by few set rules of social conduct. They also have so few rituals that their first ethnographers assumed they had no religion, or even a culture, of their own. Turnbull drew a picture of Pygmies irreverently mocking Bantu rituals and not comprehending the magic that the hunting and fertility rites of the Bantu were supposed to effect. The Pygmies are quite "secular" in their outlook, which suggests that the contrast between secular and religious has less to do with the contrast between modern and traditional than it has to do with the experience of open or closed social groups.

The contempt of external ritual forms occurs when social fluidity makes ritual communication opaque. Sociolinguistics can provide us with some explanation of the revolt against ritual in the modern West. Basil Bernstein has delineated two basic categories of speech in modern Western society:[7] (1) the *elaborated code* draws from a wide range of syntactic alternatives which require complex planning and flexible organization in order to enable a speaker to make his intentions known and to elucidate general principles; (2) the *restricted code* draws from a narrow range of syntactic alternatives which are more rigidly organized because they emerge out of, express, embellish, and reinforce the immediate social structure.

Each speech code is generated by a particular social matrix. Bernstein's research into London schools and families shows that the codes are instilled into children from earliest infancy. He describes two kinds of families which nurture two different kinds of role systems. Restricted speech codes are used in *positional* families in which the child is controlled by the building up of a sense of social patterns (often expressed in a family "hierarchy") and ascribed role categories (for example, age, sex). Elaborated speech codes are cultivated in *personal* families in which fixed roles are not cultivated, but rather the autonomy of each individual is affirmed. In such families there is no recognized hierarchy, and there is an attempt to meet the unique needs of each child by creating an entirely individual environment. Douglas asks, "How could such a child ever learn to respond to a communally exerted authority? . . . Hence some of the deafness and antipathy to ritualism in our day."[8] More and more families are adopting the personalist life style and are cultivating the elaborated code of speech. Such families seem to flourish more in the suburbs than in the cities, where ethnic subcultures preserve positional family patterns and the restricted codes of speech. It is not surprising, therefore, that ritualistic churches also flourish more in the cities than in the suburbs because urban society tends to emphasize grid more than group.

One urban ethnic group which is a principal subject of Mary Douglas's study is the Bog Irish of London. They are much like primitive ritualists in clinging tenaciously to ritual practices such as the Friday fast. Friday abstinence cannot be dismissed as a meaningless ritual just because it is observed so routinely. The meaning of the symbolic act for the Irish who observe it is that it provides *identity* for the social group, much like the kosher food laws in Judaism. Observing the Friday fast identifies one as Catholic and Irish in a largely Protestant and English society. Yet on the part of educated English Catholics there has been a discernible move away from symbolic action and toward ethical action. The Friday fast is seen less as a symbolic participation in the passion of Christ than as an opportunity to organize contributions to world hunger. And yet, as Douglas points out, "When ritualism is openly despised the philanthropic impulse is in danger of defeating itself. For it is an illusion to suppose that there can be organization without symbolic expression."[9]

Many people in our society today prefer a way of life which is "liberated" and unbounded. But drawing symbolic boundaries is a way of organizing experience and providing a structure of meanings in which individuals can relate to one another. So it is ironic that the very people today who prefer unstructured intimacy in their social relations defeat their desire to communicate through nonverbal means. "For only a ritual structure makes possible a wordless channel of communication that is not entirely incoherent."[10]

Our concern is for greater participation in liturgical action, which necessarily involves the physical body. Here, too, Mary Douglas provides some penetrating insights. She shows how the social body constrains the way the physical body is perceived in terms of grooming, feeding, sleep, exercise, and the like.[11] From early childhood on, there is a concern to coordinate the use of the body with other means of expression in social behavior. Thus, the controls exerted from the social system place limitations on the use of the body as a means of social communication. The use of one's individual body is determined to a great extent by the social body. There is no way of considering the physical body that does not involve a social dimension at the same time. If there is a concern to preserve social boundaries, there will be a concern to fix the boundaries of bodily expression. If social boundaries are fluid and flexible, the boundaries of bodily expression will also be fluid and flexible. Freedom to be relaxed and informal, therefore, is also culturally controlled.

This can be seen in the difference between worship in a liturgical church and worship in a Free Church. The Free Churches prefer a more spontaneous and emotional expression in worship. This is accomplished by sustaining a stage of religious development known as *effervescence*. To sustain effervescence, it is necessary that the level of social organization be kept low and the pattern of roles be kept sufficiently unstructured (for example, little differentiation between clergy and laity). In this social structure there is a weak control of the individual by the social grid and group. One is free to express oneself in relatively uninhibited ways. In a ritualistic church, on the other hand, there is a highly articulated social structure which includes a tight control of the individual by the social grid and group, a differentiation of social roles (clergy and laity), and an exaltation of the group over the individual. The result will be a high value placed on conscious and controlled participation in communal worship.[12]

The question for us is whether there can be a mixture of social dimensions and symbolic orders. Can conditions for effervescence be mixed with conditions for ritualism? The preference in our society recently has been for effervescent religious expression, as witness the resurgence of neo-evangelical and pentecostal churches. The mainline churches are ritualistic churches with highly articulated organizational structures and theological symbols. Is there a danger that the theological symbols would be undermined if a more effervescent social structure were allowed to flourish? On the basis of David Aberle's study of social and religious changes among the Navaho of the American Southwest, Mary Douglas has observed that when the social grip is relaxed, ritualism declines, "and with this shift of forms, a shift in doctrine appears."[13] It would seem that a symbolic system is ecological. A sense of sacramental efficacy cannot flourish in social conditions that encourage spontaneous expression, display little interest in ritual role differentiation, and lack symbolic expressions for defining insiders and outsiders. It proves to be true anthropologically as well as historically that an ordered ministry and an ordered liturgy are necessary to preserve true doctrine.

It would seem, therefore, that conditions for effervescence cannot be mixed with conditions for ritualism. An effervescent social structure will not allow a ritualistic symbolic order to flourish, and vice versa. The symbolic order is determined by the social dimension. However effervescent *preferences* can perhaps be channeled into a ritualistic system if a sufficient balance is maintained between the social grid and group so that the physical body is given room for self-expression. We will suggest some ways to do that. In the meantime, there may be a need to interest users of the elaborated code in a self-examination and inspection of their values—to cherish some and to reject others—and in the adoption of the values of the positional family, wherever these are available. This is the only way to use our knowledge to free ourselves from the grip of our symbolically impoverished cosmology so that we can learn again how to express ourselves through ritual.

Developing a Capacity to Ritualize

Ritual behavior requires the use of the body. Rationalistic people tend to be reluctant to worship with their bodies. Therefore we need to remember, as J. A. T. Robinson has written, that "man does not have a body, he *is* a body."[14] Our bodily selves are our real selves, and therefore we must communicate through our bodies. We receive information through our senses. We know that something that is seen as well as heard is conveyed more powerfully than something that is only heard. The meaning of something conveyed kinetically, that is, through bodily motion, is more powerful still. Meaning conveyed through touch and taste is more impressive than meaning expressed kinetically, visually, or audibly. And finally, meaning involving several senses at once is obviously more impressionable than meaning involving only one.

This basic physiological fact explains why liturgy was danced before it was sung and sung before it was said, and why touching and tasting have always possessed such numinous and psychological powers. "Taste and see the goodness of the Lord," said the psalmist. David danced before the ark; Ezekiel ate the scroll; John baptized with water; Jesus healed with clay and spit; Thomas touched the wounds of Christ; the early church gathered in homes to eat and drink the eucharistic bread and wine; the apostles laid on hands; medieval Christians carried the Bible, wore special clothing, inhaled incense, beat their breasts, thumbed ashes on their heads, and marched around; but we sing hymns and listen to sermons. It is a very rationalistic thing to do and quite impotent if that is all that is done in worship. We need not be afraid of sensual expression; God gave us our senses. Our suspicion of the body and our emphasis on the dualism of body and spirit is essentially a heresy. It derives from Neoplatonism, not from the Judeo-Christian heritage. Luther is reported to have made the perfect comment on the liturgical importance of the body in saying that God has given us five senses with which to worship him, and it would be sheer ingratitude to use less. Above all, the event of the incarnation validates the use of the body for the glorification of God; for all the fullness of God inhabited the body of Christ, and in Holy Baptism and in the Eucharist that body takes residence in ours in the Spirit.

We have, obviously, a lot of unlearning and reeducating to do. We have communicated the idea that the body should be kept as much out of the way of worship as possible. We have required worshipers to be someone different in worship than they are in daily life; then we are surprised that they cannot connect liturgy with life, but are passive and withdrawn at worship.

Of course, we cannot suddenly get everyone up and about, moving around and touching one another. That might even evoke latent erotic or sexual fears. In any event, we want to channel effervescent preferences into ritualistic behavior. There are traditional practices available which can be exploited: clasping hands with one another at the greeting of peace; holding hands with other people in the pew during the prayer of the church; offertory processions of the whole congregation; using real bread and a large cup at Holy Communion; blessing noncommunicants at the altar rail with a firm touch of the hand on the head. The new Liturgy of Holy Baptism is full of tactile experiences: immersion into water or having it poured over the head; putting a new white gown on the newly baptized to signify the new life in Christ; anointing the baptized with oil to signify the seal of the Spirit; handing the baptized or the sponsor a lighted candle as a sign that he or she should henceforth live a life of prayer and service. On Maundy Thursday, the foot washing can be reenacted. It could be updated by having the worship leaders wipe the shoes of the participants rather than wash their feet. On Palm Sunday and at the Easter Vigil the whole congregation can process into the church carrying palm branches or lighted candles. They might all process out of the church on Pentecost carrying evangelism tracts. On the Sunday of the Passion and during Holy Week the congregation can read the lines of the crowd in the passion narratives. On occasion, a chancel drama might take the place of the sermon (for example, on Epiphany), and liturgical dance can be employed to interpret hymns or Scripture readings. Agape meals might be held on some weekday commemorations in the form of a businessmen's breakfast following a communion service, or as a pot luck dinner preceding a communion service.

Paul Hoon encourages these and other liturgical actions for theological, psychological, and spiritual reasons.[15] A theological dimension is, in any event, needed so that worship does not degenerate into activities for the sake of activities. But it is also important to affirm that God's action occurs in the context of human action. His grace comes through a ritual washing and a shared meal. His sacramental action occurs in, with, and through our sacrificial action. As this happens, it is God himself who determines the nature of the action in which we are engaged. The presence of the God of love who humbled himself unto obedient death on the cross in order to reconcile us to himself summons us to bend the knee in repentance and extend the arms in adoration.

As we do this, we know that our bodily actions will also determine our emotions more than our emotions will determine our actions. To paraphrase a saying of Friedrich von Hügel's, we worship God not only because we fear, love, and trust him above all things, but *also in order to* fear, love, and trust him above all things. We can seldom will ourselves to *feel* a certain way, but we can will ourselves to *act*, and actions that are repeated can summon attitudes that once attended them. Original feelings can be reawakened. As Margaret Mead suggests, it is one of the functions of ritual to give people "access to intensity of feeling at times when responsiveness is muted . . . to lift people above the dullness that inevitably follows on moments of high feeling and to reinstate the high ecstacy that is so transient an experience."[16]

Liturgical action thus has a formative role to play. It provides a discipline for the individual Christian and the whole congregation because repetitive behavior is a conditioning process. It is a liturgical act to get out of bed on Sunday morning in order to assemble and celebrate with the congregation. Alexander Schmemann writes that the liturgical journey into the dimension of the kingdom begins when Christians leave home to go to church. "They leave, indeed, their life in this present and concrete world, and whether they have to drive fifteen miles or walk a few blocks, a sacramental act is already taking place, an act which is the very condition of everything else that is to happen. For they are now on their way to *constitute the Church,* or to be more exact, to be transformed into the Church of God."[17]

The conditioning process of liturgical action also continues after the service when liturgical action is turned into ethical action. The Word and Sacrament not only draw us into the kingdom of Christ but also propel us into the kingdom of this world. The conditioning which occurs through the combined impact of the many liturgical actions must surely have some effect on a person's subconscious responses. As Paul Hoon suggests:

> A worshipper may bring more courage to the threatening changes of history if he has regularly knelt—as Luther advised us to do—at the words of the Creed marking the invasion of the Divine into history: *homo factus est . . .* He can appraise both the good and evil of secular influences hourly beating upon his consciousness if he has regularly signed his existence with the sign of the cross. And he may more likely stand up for the gospel in the ambiguous ethical decisions he must make in his life in the world if he has stood for the gospel in his worship.[18]

This move from liturgy to life does not negate a comparable move from life to liturgy; indeed, the gathering and scattering nature of the liturgical assembly suggests Christians will bring moral and social concerns to church with them and be dismissed from the liturgy of Word and Sacrament to "carry out" the liturgy of mission. Such an observation suggests that worship should be seen as a source for ethical response as well as for theological reflection.

the world view of WORSHIP

Liturgy and Theology

We have been doing liturgical theology all along. When we make decisions about the language and actions of worship we are making theological decisions, either because the practice of worship will inform and influence theology or because theological *a priori* governs the practical decisions that are made. There has always been a reciprocal relationship between the *lex orandi* ("the rule of prayer") and the *lex credendi* ("the rule of belief").[1] In the ancient church, prayers addressed to Christ in Christian devotion influenced the development of Christological dogma. On the other hand, Arians made use of the mediatory role of Christ in public prayer ("through Jesus Christ our Lord") in order to defend their subordinationist Christology. Josef Jungmann points out that it was in response to this Arian appeal to the church's prayer that Catholics in Spain and Gaul expanded the concluding formula by adding "who lives and reigns with the Father and the Holy Spirit, one God, now and forever."[2] Or again, Irenaeus turned to the Eucharist for "proof" against the Gnostics that the one God and Father of Jesus Christ is the creator of the material world, which is good and not intrinsically evil. On the other hand, the emphasis on the goodness of the material creation contributed to the development of the offertory, that is, the actual offering of the material elements to God in a sacrifice of praise and thanksgiving.[3] In the light of this offertory development it is noteworthy that the preferred term for the Lord's Supper, which had been *eucharistia* in the second century, became *oblatio* in the third and fourth centuries.

Protestants have been especially wary about viewing the liturgy as the norm, source, or authority for doctrinal development. In particular, it is evident that Marian devotion over many centuries contributed to the formulation of the dogmas of the immaculate conception of Mary (1854) and her bodily assumption into heaven (1950). Protestants might point out that these dogmas would never have been promulgated if Scripture alone had been taken as the source and norm of both doctrine and practice. Yet the matter is not quite so simple. Holy Scripture is read and expounded in the context of public worship. In fact, it was such a use that led to the canonization of biblical books. Moreover, the use of Scripture in worship, as well as the liturgical provenance of some biblical books, provides a key to biblical interpretation. Furthermore, public worship is not only what the church does, but also what God does through the proclamation of the Word, the administration of the sacraments, and the workings of the Holy Spirit to inspire prayer and prophecy. If worship is an encounter with God, that makes it a source of doctrine, since doctrine is an articulation of the experience of God's work of creation, redemption, and sanctification. If some theological difficulties are raised by such doctrinal formulations as the Marian dogmas mentioned above, this is not so much a problem with the *lex orandi* as with the way in which the *lex credendi* is specified. Indeed, Marian piety down through the ages has served as a way of safeguarding the incarnation, as witness the role of the concept of the *theotokos* in the christological controversies leading to the Chalcedonian formulation. The problem was the dogmatizing of piety. The same might be said of the dogma of transubstantiation as a specific articulation of the eucharistic piety of the Western Middle Ages. We might want to affirm the *lex credendi* embodied in the *lex orandi* of medieval eucharistic devotion without affirming the dogmatic conclusions drawn from that piety.

If worship is a source of doctrine, if liturgical data provides grist for theological reflection, then perhaps what is needed is a bridge between the raw data and the dogmatic or systematic formulation. Liturgical theology does that bridgework by reflecting on the meanings of liturgical rites, texts, and practices. If we take worship seriously as a source for theological reflection, what visions emerge of man as a worshiping being, of the kind of God who is the object of worship, and of the kind of ethical response which appropriately follows the encounter with this God in worship?

Geoffrey Wainwright points out in his systematic theology entitled *Doxology* that we see man in worship realizing his vocation to be in communion with God.[4] This is an eschatological foretaste of "the chief end of man," as defined in the Westminster Shorter Catechism, "to glorify God and enjoy him forever." Or, as Alexander Schmemann puts it, man is *homo adorans*, "the one for whom worship is the essential act which both 'posits' his humanity and fulfills it."[5] This opens up a sacramental world view which regards the world as an epiphany of God, as the place of his revelation, presence, and power. Such a world view may be contrasted with that of secularism, which Schmemann defines as "a negation of worship." Secularism is not so much a negation of God or of religion as it is a negation of man as a worshiping being, who has what Rudolf Otto called "creature feelings" of awe and fascination in the presence of the Holy.

This point of view may seem to emphasize the verticality of worship since it sees worship first and foremost as an encounter with the Holy. It recognizes that worshipers come together primarily to be in communion with God. But in that divine presence they also discover one another. They recognize an interpersonal relationship which is qualitatively different from the relationships experienced in "this world." In the process of this discovery of one another, the verticality of worship is joined to the horizontal plane, which graphically results in the sign of the cross—the aegis under which specifically Christian worship takes place.

We would not at all want to deny that worshipers should cultivate an interior disposition of communion with God. But communion with God in public worship is expressed more especially through external means. The worshiper encounters God through public reading, preaching, water, bread, and wine. Yet just here we would have to observe the use of these earthly elements as the means of grace. This observation has led Christians to affirm that God is involved in the nitty-gritty affairs of life. His willingness to intervene in human history caused the incarnation and crucifixion of his only begotten Son. The worship of such a God in the Spirit of Christ cannot be an escape from this world. It is rather the affirmation of this world as the theater of grace, as the place of encounter with God, as the means of communion with him. As James White put it, "To be truly spiritual is to be truly worldly."[6]

It is this affirmation of the worldly in the midst of otherworldly worship that secularization has accomplished. Secularization may indeed be a healthy corrective of a sacralization which degenerates into clericalism or political quietism. But it also runs the risk of degenerating into secularism, which in its extreme manifestations prizes worldly success (for example, pulling oneself up by one's own boot-straps) and collapses transcendence into immanence.

The problem of secular man as he relates to liturgy is his basic inability to worship, to let himself go in order "to glorify God, and to enjoy him forever" (in the words of the Westminster Shorter Catechism). This is seen, as Schmemann points out, "in his naive conviction that worship, as everything else in the world, can be a rational construction, the result of planning, 'exchange of views,' and discussion."[7] Typical of this approach has been the discussion about finding new symbols, as if they can be created by a committee. Symbols are more than audio-visual aids for communicating ideas. "A sign," wrote the psychologist C. G. Jung, "is an analogous or abbreviated expression of a *known* thing. But a symbol is always the best possible expression of a relatively *unknown* fact, a fact, however, which is nonetheless recognized or postulated as existing."[8] To put it another way, signs *signify*; symbols *reveal* or disclose meaning in a way which expands one's frame of reference. This does not mean that signs are of less value than symbols; they are simply different. The bread and wine of the Eucharist, for example, are proclaimed to be signs of the body and blood of Christ. A doctrine of the real presence holds that the signs correspond exactly with what they signify. But the *way* in which communion is administered is a symbolic act because it is capable of manifold possibilities of interpretation and affects people in ways which cannot precisely be spelled out. But just because symbols are capable of manifold interpretation does not mean that they can be invented. A symbol is not invented; it is recognized and usually communally recognized.

Worship is a symbolic activity. It has meaning in itself which is conveyed simply by doing it. There is a sense in which it is bastardized when it is *used* to further some other purpose which is not intrinsic to the act of worship itself. It has been so used in recent years to further institutional ecclesiastical programs in such areas of parish life as education, evangelism, and stewardship. There is a relationship between worship and education: the words and actions of the liturgy are capable of instructing in Christian doctrine and life. There is a relationship between worship and evangelism: well done liturgy can make a positive experiential impact on people. There is a relationship between worship and stewardship: participation in the liturgy affords Christians an opportunity to employ their God-given gifts to the glory of God and the edification of their fellow believers. But these are byproducts of worship. Furthering institutional programs is not what worship is all about. Utilitarianism is a corruption of worship. It could be debated whether worship should ever be used as a means to an end rather than an end in itself. It is, after all, first and foremost an encounter with the living God through proclamation of the Word and administration of the sacraments. It is the occasion to receive God's gracious gifts and the opportunity for the people of God to respond to these gifts with their sacrifices of prayer, praise, and thanksgiving.

This suggests that worship is composed of dimensions which the Lutheran tradition, following Philip Melanchthon, has designated as "sacramental" and "sacrificial." In a major study of the doctrine of Christian worship Peter Brunner called these two dimensions "worship as a service of God to the congregation" and "worship as the congregation's service before God."[9] He is careful not to fall into the trap into which older dogmaticians fell when they proceeded to label each part of the liturgy either "sacramental" or "sacrificial." Such labeling determined the rubrics of posture. If a part of the service was considered to be "sacramental" the minister faced the people; if it was considered to be "sacrificial" the minister faced the altar. A free-standing altar, of course, blows such distinctions to smithereens. Furthermore, there is no indication that Melanchthon would have used these categories in such a mechanical way. They are rather two dimensions of worship that occur simultaneously. This is clear even in Melanchthon's presentation in Article XXIV of the Apology to the Augsburg Confession.[10] We would think, for example, that preaching is a sacramental act since it is the Word of God addressed to the congregation; but Melanchthon lists it among the "sacrifices of praise." So, too, the eucharistic prayer would seem to be a sacrificial act; yet from the earliest days of Christian worship it has served as a proclamation of the mighty acts of God.

The sacrificial aspect of worship has received little emphasis in the Protestant traditions. However much the reformers differed in their understanding of the eucharistic presence of Christ, they were unanimous in their condemnation of the "sacrifice of the Mass." Luther saw in the Mass-sacrifice the root of all the false understandings and abuses in connection with the sacrament of the altar: the mechanical notion of liturgical acts in the doctrine of *ex opere op-*

erato, Mass-stipends, the multiplication of private Masses, especially votive masses for the dead, infrequent communion, and so forth. He complained that one heard only about what "we offer" and "these gifts," but never about the sacrifice which Christ performed on our behalf. In reaction he struck from the Mass everything which "smacked and savored of sacrifice": all the offertory prayers and the prayers of the eucharistic canon other than the preface, the Words of Institution, and the Sanctus.[11] The other reformers followed suit in characteristic fashion. Zwingli wrote another "canon." Calvin left the institution narrative standing by itself as a "warrant" for the celebration and replaced the prayers with exhortation and instruction addressed to the people. Cranmer stuck close to the structure of the Roman Canon in the 1549 *Book of Common Prayer,* but changed the emphasis so that what is offered is not Christ but our own prayers of praise and thanksgiving in remembrance of Christ's "one oblation once offered."[12]

While the Protestant tradition has been understandably wary of the sacrificial dimension of worship, it cannot be ignored. Indeed, as Peter Brunner suggests, it is distinguished by eschatological validity. Preaching of the gospel and administration of the sacraments will cease: but the acclamation, praise, and adoration of God will continue forever. The worship of faltering earthly pilgrims is, in Brunner's words, "the beginning of the eternal glorification of the Triune God."[13] This is most directly expressed in the gathering of the faithful on the Lord's Day, the eschatological day of resurrection and new creation (the fathers called it the "eighth day"), to celebrate the eschatological banquet of which the risen Lord is both host and food. In the Anaphora or Great Thanksgiving the faithful are invited to: "lift up your hearts," to ascend to where Christ is in heaven and to join in the heavenly worship singing the thrice-holy hymn. The introductory section of the eucharistic prayer is called the Preface, but "preface" does not here mean "introduction." It comes from the Latin *praefari,* which means "to pray aloud." Traditionally, the Preface has been sung: however, angels and archangels are not the sort of beings we prosaically number among our praying company. The text of the Preface and Sanctus is ecstatic; it invites the presiding minister and celebrating people to break into chant.

Music engenders a sense of eternity, a harmonic blending of past, present, and future. It is from the perspective of eternity that we see heaven and earth full of the glory of the Lord. It is in the presence of the eternal God that we remember all that he has done for us and give thanks for all his benefits, especially for the act of salvation in Christ, of which the bread and wine we offer become the sign and seal. God has given us all things, especially the gift of life. It is not surprising that the gift of new life comes to us as food—"This is my body. This is my blood." Generations of theologians have asked how this can be and have tried to explain it. From an eschatological perspective it suffices to confess with St. Ambrose of Milan that the word of Christ is effective for all eternity; for as cocreator with the Father "He spoke and it was made, he commanded and it was created." And the Spirit who transformed chaos now transforms bread and wine and the assembled people and thereby transforms the church into the body of Christ.

In the Spirit of Christ, given in baptism, we have ascended into heaven without ever leaving the world behind. The "now/not yet" tension of fulfillment/anticipation in the eucharistic meal is expressed by intercessions in the eucharistic prayer and by the petitions of the Lord's Prayer in which Jesus taught his disciples to pray for those things which signify the presence of the kingdom of God in this world: the hallowing of God's name, the rule of his will on earth, the forgiveness of sins, and deliverance from the apocalyptic tribulation that precedes the coming of the kingdom in power and glory. Even the petition for "daily bread" can be understood as a yearning for the antepast of heaven, of which the Lord's Supper is a foretaste. In the Orthodox liturgy, so strong is the sense of the presence of eternity in the eucharistic celebration that the "spiritual worship" of the Eucharist is offered "for those resting in the faith, the forefathers, fathers, patriarchs, prophets, apostles, preachers, evangelists, martyrs, confessors, ascetics, and for every holy soul who has run the course in the faith—especially for our all-holy, spotless, most highly blessed and glorious Lady the Mother of God and ever-virgin Mary." The earthly church eats the eucharistic meal in the company of heaven.

Evelyn Underhill wrote that the essence of worship "in all its grades and kinds" is the "response of the creature to the Eternal."[14] If this is so, the highest form of response is the eucharistic sacrifice. To be sure, the community of the new covenant no longer had a specific sacrificial cult. But this did not eliminate the idea of sacrifice from Christian worship; rather, it broadened and deepened it. Sacramental assimilation to the death of Christ (Rom. 6:4–6) meant that the pattern of Christ's passion was to be reproduced in the lives of his followers (Gal. 2:20). Indeed, St. Paul could assert, "Now I rejoice in my sufferings for your sake, and in my flesh I complete what is lacking in Christ's afflictions for the sake of his body, that is, the church" (Col. 1:24). The fact that redemption in Christ is a pure gift in no way excludes human works in the living of the redeemed life. Such works are an expression of the Holy Spirit—who activates faith into deeds of love—in the lives of believers.

Sacramental assimilation to the death of Christ is the basis of Christian asceticism. " I pommel my body and subdue it, lest after preaching to others I myself should be disqualified" (1 Cor. 9:27). St. Paul runs the race of life in order to win the crown of glory at the end (1 Cor. 9:24–27). It is from this comparison of Christian life to athletic training that we get the term "asceticism." This training or discipline lays the foundation for Christian ethics. "'All things are lawful,' but not all things are helpful. 'All things are lawful,' but not all things build up. Let no one seek his own good, but the good of his neighbor" (1 Cor. 10:23).

It is this whole life of self-surrender to the will of God that is the living out of sacramental assimilation to Christ, and the foundation for the eucharistic sacrifice. As that later Pauline theologian St. Augustine of Hippo expressed in *The City of God*: "the whole redeemed community, that is to say, the congregation and fellowship of the saints, is offered to God as a universal sacrifice, through the great Priest who offered himself in his suffering for us—so that we might be the body of so great a Head—under 'the form of a servant.'"[15] The sacrificial life of the church, which Christ offers to the Father, is viewed as the fulfillment of the pure oblation of the Gentiles in the messianic age prophesied in Mal. 1:11, 14.

This "pure oblation" (*Didache* 14) is publicly expressed in the great prayer of thanksgiving over the bread and the cup. The praise of God in this prayer is a public acknowledgment of his mighty acts of creation and redemption, of which the bread and wine are a tangible symbol.[16] In the ancient anaphoras, the verbalization of this offering occurred between the remembrance of God's saving acts and the supplication for the gift of communion (often expressed as an invocation of the Holy Spirit). Thus, in the Anaphora of Hippolytus (ca. 215), in the version found in the Ministers Edition of the *Lutheran Book of Worship*, we have:[17]

> Remembering [*Memores*], then,
>   his death and resurrection,
>   we lift [*offerimus*] this bread and cup
>   before you,
>   giving you thanks that
>   you have made us worthy
>   to stand before you
>   and to serve you
>   as your priestly people.
> And we ask you [*petimus*]:
>   Send your Spirit
>   upon these gifts of your Church;
>   gather into one
>   all who share this bread and wine;
>   fill us with your Holy Spirit
>   to establish our faith in truth,
>   that we may praise
>   and glorify you
>   through your Son Jesus Christ.

The same structure is fleshed out in the later Anaphora of St. John Chrysostom, which is still in regular use in the Byzantine churches.[18]

> *Remembering*, therefore, this precept of salvation and everything that was done for our sake, the cross, the tomb, the resurrection on the third day, the ascension into heaven, the enthronement at the right hand, the second and glorious coming again, *we offer* You your own, from what is your own, in all and for the sake of all.

> Moreover, *we offer* you this spiritual and unbloody worship, and *we ask and pray and entreat*: send down your Holy Spirit upon us and upon these gifts here offered. And make this bread the precious body of your Christ. And that which is in the chalice the precious blood of your Christ. Changing them by your Holy Spirit.

> So that, to those who partake of them, they may be for the cleansing of the soul, for the remission of sins, for the fellowship of your Holy Spirit, for the fullness of the kingdom of heaven, for intimate confidence in You, and not for judgment or condemnation.

The same concept can be seen in the Roman Canon, although Jungmann points out that the direction of the epiclesis has been reversed so that the Spirit does not descend on the gifts but an angel carries the gifts to the heavenly altar.[19]

Father, *we celebrate the memory* of Christ, your Son.
We, your people and your ministers,
recall his passion,
his resurrection from the dead,
and his ascension into glory;
and from the many gifts you have given us
we offer to you, God of glory and majesty,
this holy and perfect sacrifice:
the bread of life
and the cup of eternal salvation.

Look with favor on these offerings
and accept them as once you accepted
the gifts of your servant Abel,
the sacrifice of Abraham, our father in faith,
and the bread and wine offered by your priest Melchisedech.

Almighty God,
we pray that your angel may take this sacrifice
to your altar in heaven.
Then, as we receive from this altar
the sacred body and blood of your Son,
let us be filled with every grace and blessing.

What is being offered? What is the content and meaning of the
offering? Each of these texts, originating in sources which are roughly
two centuries apart from one another (third, fifth and seventh centuries), speak literally of the offering of the bread and cup, which
represent material gifts taken from all that God has given to us. Such
an offering is a thanks offering, expressing gratitude for all that God
has given to us. At the same time, these gifts function as signs of
our self-offering. The inclusion of Melchizedek among the patriarchs
who offer sacrifices in faith in the Roman Canon may even be a way
of alluding to the pure offering of the Gentiles prophesied by Malachi.
This metaphor served as a way of describing the eucharistic sacrifice
in texts ranging from the *Didache* to Augustines's *City of God.*
At the same time, the fathers speak of the bread and cup as the
"likeness" or "figure" of the body and blood of Christ. This is sugges-
tive of Christ's sacrifice which he presents to the Father on our
behalf.

It is obvious that the language of sacrifice in the patristic texts is
polysemous. It is only when theologians began trying to specify a
"moment of consecration" effecting a conversion of the bread and

wine into the body and blood of Christ that difficulties arose. All the texts we have cited follow the institution narrative in the anaphoral structure. When the Western church associated the conversion of the gifts with the proclamation of the words of Christ, as we already see in the writings of Ambrose of Milan, the idea could be conveyed that the body and blood of Christ are being offered to God the Father. This notion was combined with the concept of the votive mass (that is, the offering of the Eucharist for special intentions), which became increasingly popular after the sixth century. Working from such a development, medieval theologians developed the concept that the authority of the priest is to offer the sacrifice of the Mass for the living and the dead. This was combined with a rather lucrative source of stipends, so it is easy to understand how the whole system aroused the ire of the reformers in the sixteenth century. With Luther we would agree that it is a blasphemous notion that the body and blood of Christ can be offered to God for special intentions. Such a view reverses the "direction" of the sacrament and obscures its character as God's gift to his people. None of the patristic texts speak of offering the body and blood of Christ. Therefore, if we were able to put aside the scholastic concern for the "moment of consecration" and return to the patristic data, it might be possible to break through the Reformation deadlock on the issue of eucharistic sacrifice.[20]

There are important pastoral, ethical, and missional reasons for coming to terms with the eucharistic sacrifice as the ancient church understood it. It clarifies the relationship between public worship and the activities of daily life. In the theology of the fathers we find no dichotomy between prayer and action, liturgy and ethics, worship and mission. Each informs the other in a holistic view of the life of faith in Christian community. Certainly the Christian transformation of the notion of sacrifice had ethical consequences in terms of the surrender of oneself to the service of God. We have seen the relationship between eucharistic sacrifice and asceticism in the ancient church and in the next chapter we will explore the relationship between Eucharist and martyrdom. In the same way, there is a discernible correlation today between a more action-oriented worship which culminates in the eucharistic celebration and a heightened Christian consciousness of participation in public events and agitation for a freer and more open society. The intersection of worship and daily life, of worship and ethical response, has found a locus especially at the point of intercessory prayer and offertory, which have been located back to back in the liturgical tradition. In new Episcopalian, Lutheran, and Methodist liturgies the greeting of peace intrudes between the general intercessions and the offertory. The greeting suggests that the concern for reconciliation ought to characterize the community that dares to exercise the royal priesthood of the people of God by offering the world to God in a sacrifice of love and praise.

The offertory action needs to be seen as *the* expression of eucharistic sacrifice. As we have suggested, that self-offering of the church was originally expressed in the eucharistic prayer. Subsequently, offertory rites have evolved that serve in a sense to emphasize by duplication the presentation of the self-offering of the church to God the Father, on the basis of the church's relationship in the Spirit to Jesus Christ, whose sacrifice the Father has already accepted. There has been an interest in recent years in reviving the ancient offertory procession of the faithful, in which all sorts of gifts are brought to the altar—the bread and wine for the Eucharist as well as the money offerings of the people and, on occasion, even food and clothing for the needy. It is particularly at the offertory that the relationship between cult and culture must be more precisely defined, since it is culture itself that is being offered to God: for example, food, implements, utensils, works of art, language, and so forth.[21] What does it mean, in defining the relationship between cult and culture, that we offer to God cereals and grapes—that have been manufactured into some forms of bread and wine, which are contained in baskets, cruets, chalices, and patens made by artisans of straw, glass, metals, or earthenware—along with tokens of the results of our exchange of goods and services, while musicians render choral or instrumental compositions? Do we see culture in terms of the essential goodness of creation or in terms of distortion symbolized by the fall? Does redemption take place within the cultural process or apart from it?

Worship and Culture

One of the most thorough analyses of the possible relationships between the gospel and culture is H. Richard Niebuhr's *Christ and Culture*. Niebuhr's typologies have been applied to the specific relationship between worship and culture by Geoffrey Wainwright.[22] These typologies are (in the order we shall consider them): Christ of culture, Christ against culture, Christ above culture, Christ and culture in paradox, and Christ the transformer of culture.

The first two types represent a rather simplistic approach: secular culture is either viewed as essentially good and is therefore to be embraced in a rather knee-jerk fashion, or else it is viewed as essentially corrupt and is to be rejected. The one position represents accommodation to culture; the other a countercultural stance.

In an essay entitled "Christian Worship or Cultural Incantation?" Brian Spinks saw cultural accommodation in the work of many liturgical committees which conducted opinion polls among the users of their trial rites in an effort to ensure that contemporary world views and life styles are expressed in new liturgical rites and texts.[23] There is always the danger of capitulating to the latest cultural fad without giving it a second thought. But surveys have also produced responses from those who opt for a countercultural stance by pitting some kind of idealized ecclesiastical culture against a secular one. This type of party in every church helped to apply the brakes to a facile accommodation to current cultural trends.

Neither one of these approaches seems adequate to the task of relating worship to culture in a situation in which the church is neither in a position of cultural dominance nor of persecution. Niebuhr's three other typologies present this relationship in a more complex light.

The "Christ above culture" model received archetypal expression in the medieval synthesis of Thomas Aquinas, in which grace lifts up culture to perfection rather than accommodating to it as it is or seeking to destroy it.[24] The problem with this model is that historically conditioned cultural expressions can become absolutized to the prohibition of utilizing cultural expressions from other times and places. For example, many people think Gothic when they think of church buildings, forgetting that in the twelfth and thirteenth centuries Gothic was simply the architectural style of the age. And yet, it is a common experience that Gothic architecture may be the least conducive to housing contemporary liturgical celebrations because it tends to scatter the congregation rather than gather it together. The major objection to the "synthesis" model of "Christ above culture" is that it does not face up to the limitations and liabilities of human achievement. This objection is strongly voiced by the "dualists."

Niebuhr calls the dualist view "Christ and culture in paradox."

This view sees human culture and society subject to God's "left hand" while the church and the spiritual life is subject to God's "right hand." This view is archetypally represented by Luther and in the two kingdoms doctrine.[25] Perhaps the most positive aspect of this approach is that it sees both cult and culture as existing under the rule of God. The family, the state, and the arts have a rather high position in Luther's doctrine of the orders of creation. Such a view made possible the doctrine of lay vocation, provided impetus for the development of the nation-state, and demonstrated an openness to contemporary music and the arts. The liability of this "dualist" stance, however, is that God's one hand may not know what the other hand is doing.[26] Society goes one way while the church goes another. It has been observed that the two kingdoms doctrine came to disastrous consequence in the twentieth century with the Christian toleration of fascist and totalitarian states. We have also noted the increasing secularization of music and the arts since the time of the Enlightenment in relation to the increasing impoverishment of Christian worship and the inability of the Christian cult to make an impact on culture. Some have seen the recent emergence of rock musicals such as *Jesus Christ Superstar* and *Godspell*—or, in a more classical vein, a work such as Benjamin Britten's *War Requiem* with its interplay between the texts of the requiem mass and Wilfred Owen's agnostic war poems—as a possible bridge between cult and culture. The fruition of such hopes depends on how deep the chasm is between Christian worship and contemporary Western culture. In any event, the dualist approach is not likely to overcome this break because it basically leaves culture and society untouched and unchanged.

So we turn, finally, to the fifth model presented by Niebuhr: "Christ the transformer of culture." This scheme has appealed to modern liturgical theologians, such as Geoffrey Wainwright, who notes that "it rests on a positive doctrine of creation and the incarnation, while yet admitting the radical corruption of humanity."[27] Corruption implies the need for purification, rebirth, transformation, but not the need for replacement. In this fifth model by Niebuhr the pattern of death and resurrection can be applied to human culture, and baptism is the appropriate liturgical model. Of course, there are initiatory rites in all societies which utilize the pattern of death and resurrection, and these symbols are indeed universal in human experience. But to "christianize" them means to understand these symbols in reference to the kingdom of God, which has been inaugurated in the death and resurrection of Jesus Christ.

The model of transformation suggests that any natural symbol can be baptized for use in the Christian cult. Any cultural expression or social institution can be "christianized," as it were. Niebuhr took as representatives of the "conversionist" model John Wesley and F. D. Maurice, both of whom were churchmen who broke through the cultic barriers erected by the church of their time in order to reach out to those in society who had become estranged from the church.[28] He placed them in the company of Augustine of Hippo, who held to the basic goodness of culture while realistically recognizing the corruption resulting from the fall. Augustine knew that human culture needs to be redeemed before the city of man can become the city of God, and that this redemption could only be an act of divine grace and not a human achievement. This means that there cannot be an easy correlation between the Christian cult and the culture of this world. Augustine had to warn Christians not to identify the kingdom of God with *Romanitas*. Likewise, as Nicholas Berdyaev wrote in our own century, "the Christian idea of the kingdom of God and the eschatological consciousness have no connection with the idolizing of historical sanctities, such as the conservative tradition of authoritarianism, monarchy, nationalism, family property, as well as of revolutionary democratic socialist sanctities."[29] While cultural expressions and social institutions can be "christianized" to the extent that Christians practice or participate in them, there can ultimately be no such thing as a Christian culture, a Christian society, a Christian state, a Christian family, a Christian economic system, and so forth, in anything other than a sociological sense. Yet each of these is capable of being transformed into signs pointing to the reality of the divine kingdom.

Nevertheless, the gospel of the kingdom of God has been able to bring about transformation in all areas of culture and in social and personal life. It has done so imperceptibly and inwardly, for where the kingdom comes with observation it is a snare and a delusion. One can imagine the hidden power of grace in Holy Communion to break down barriers between those who commune as one body in Christ. Or again, the reverential care with which the consecrated elements are disposed might help to alter attitudes toward the care of the earth in such matters as the use of soil as a chemical waste dump or the use of a lake as a source of water with which to wash out oil bunkers. In any event, the realization of a correlation between liturgy and ethics ultimately depends on the transformation of the individual worshiper. For the gospel appeals first of all to the inner, spiritual person and not to the outer, social being. What is experienced in the hearing of the Word and reception of the sacraments is the awakening and regeneration of the spiritual life, which has ramifications for the social life (as the example of evangelical Pietism testifies). It is well, therefore, that we consider in the next chapter the relationship between liturgy and spiritual life since spiritual regeneration is the basis of " the ethics of creativeness" which relate to the life of the kingdom of God as it is lived proleptically in this world.[30]

7

the piety of WORSHIP

The Estrangement of Piety from Liturgy

There has been an intense quest for spirituality in recent years. Some may interpret this as a reaction to the apparent derailment of the hopes of the 1960s or as a romantic response to a classicist life style in a technocratic society. A study of the history of spirituality shows that there is a search for new forms of devotional expression or piety during periods of drastic historical change. It is not surprising, therefore, that some of the most creative periods in the history of Christian spirituality occurred during moments of historical transition—that is, the period of late antiquity when the classical culture of the Roman Empire was collapsing along with the Roman state, the late Middle Ages when medieval society was experiencing some decisive economic and political changes, and, if we may be prophetic, in this postmodern era.

Two of the constant forms of spirituality are asceticism and mysticism. In Christian terms, asceticism is the organization of life in conformity with following the way of the cross. Mysticism is the experience of oneness with God through Christ in the Holy Spirit. These dimensions of expressing the divine-human relationship were already articulated by St. Paul, as in Rom. 8:5–11. In this passage he urges those who are "in Christ" to struggle against "the flesh" (that is, the life style of this world) in order to remain in union with the Spirit of the risen Christ who "dwells in you."

Forms of asceticism and mysticism have undergone transformation throughout the history of Christian spirituality. When the age of persecution was ended, and the church was settling down for the long haul through history in collusion with the Roman state, and the eschatological fervor of primitive Christianity was diminishing, new forms of asceticism arose in the hermetism of the desert fathers, and new forms of mysticism arose in the Neoplatonic-inspired doctrine of spiritual progress promulgated in the fifth century by Evagrius Ponticus and in the anonymous writings ascribed to Dionysius the Pseudo-Areopagite. Both of these forms of spirituality were cultivated in the monasteries of late antiquity and in the Middle Ages.

For the rank-and-file Christians, however, public worship has served as the primary vehicle for expressing devotion to God. Ascetic practices such as fasting were related to preparation for baptism and Holy Communion. Eucharistic devotion itself was a means of experiencing the immediacy of the Lord's presence and being one with him. The mystical dimension of the sacraments (also called "mysteries") is evident in what the church has said about them: they effect union with Christ.

Nevertheless, we have inherited a situation in which little relationship is seen between liturgy and personal devotion. Except perhaps in the Free Church tradition, where public worship actually resembles a kind of devotional exercise done corporately, there has been a widespread feeling that liturgy actually gets in the way of devotion.[1] The time for expressing devotion is before or after the service, but not during it. This attitude prevails in spite of the fact that many of the texts of the liturgy, such as litanies, canticles, and even the Creed, became a part of the liturgy for devotional reasons.

How did it happen that liturgy and piety became estranged from one another? There are historical reasons for this which are important to understand if we ever want to cultivate a genuinely liturgical spirituality, that is, a way of experiencing and expressing one's relationship with God through the vehicle of the liturgy. The reason for wanting to cultivate a liturgical spirituality is because it is preeminently a *churchly* spirituality. It is a way of experiencing and expressing the divine-human relationship within the context of the community of faith.

In looking at the relationship between liturgy and piety, we must begin with that period in which liturgy and piety were solidly unified and then trace the relationship through the various periods of church history, noting the factors that contributed to the divorce.

Abbot Gabriel Braso of Montserrat has written, "the common spirituality of the Christians has been subjected to the fluctuations of the various facts and circumstances which have contributed to forming its history."[2] It is generally conceded that the period of antiquity (up to the pontificate of St. Gregory the Great [590–604]) constitutes a high point in the history of spirituality. Especially in the age of persecution there was a remarkable correlation between public worship and personal Christian life. One might say that public worship was a celebration of personal Christian life. The various Acts of the Martyrs are superb testimonies of the ecclesial spirit which dominated the thinking of ancient Christians. The Letters of St. Ignatius of Antioch to various churches were written as the bishop was being taken in custody to Rome for certain death (ca. A.D. 110). In his Letter to the Romans he actually expresses a desire for martyrdom which many modern Christians would find shocking. In a sense, it was an impatience for eschatological perfection: "Let me be fodder for wild beasts—that is how I can get to God."[3] Martyrdom was the highest form of the imitation of Christ: "By our patience, let us show we are brothers, intent on imitating the Lord, seeing which of us can be the more wronged, robbed, and despised."[4] Being an imitator of Christ is not only for the sake of "attaining Christ," but also of "being found in Christ." This identification with Christ was associated with the Eucharist and with church structure, which Ignatius mentions in one breath. "Be careful, then, to observe a single Eucharist. For there is one flesh of our Lord, Jesus Christ, and one cup of his blood that makes *us* one, and one altar, just as there is one bishop along with the presbytery and the deacons, my fellow slaves. In that way whatever you do is in line with God's will."[5]

In the Eucharist we receive Christ—the Christ of the passion who became the risen Lord. In receiving the eucharistic bread and cup we enter into the process that brought him to resurrection. The implications of this are explicit in the remarkable Martyrdom of Polycarp. In his prayer at the stake, Polycarp is reported to have said: "I bless thee, because thou hast deemed me worthy of this day and hour, to take my part in the number of the martyrs, in the cup of thy Christ, for 'resurrection to eternal life' of soul and body in the immortality of the Holy Spirit."[6] The witness reported that Polycarp was in the midst of the flames, "not as burning flesh, but as bread baking or as gold and silver refined in a furnace. And we perceived such a sweet aroma as the breath of incense or some other precious spice."[7] Here was a eucharistic sacrifice; that is, what was given in the Eucharist was fulfilled in martyrdom, just as martyrdom before baptism was reckoned as baptism in one's own blood.[8] Origen developed the theme of the Eucharist as a preparation for martyrdom in his *Exhortations to Martyrdom.* Martyrdom is drinking the cup that Jesus drank to the full (Matt. 20:22). There were some awaiting martyrdom who would take no food but the Eucharist. As Louis Bouyer points out in his history of spirituality, the question was raised as to what good these preparations were if martyrdom was not attained.[9] Origen proposed the idea of an unbloody or spiritual martyrdom. This resulted in the development of ascetic discipline as a substitute for martyrdom, especially once the age of persecution was ended.

In the discussion of martyrdom in the ancient church, we see no dichotomy between liturgy and piety; they are one and the same. This was because of the corporate consciousness of the ancient church, which was manifested in congregational life and liturgical practice. It was in the liturgical assembly, and not sequestered in an inquiry classroom, that the catechumens were taught the faith and formed in the Christian life style. The rites of Christian initiation were typically celebrated annually at the paschal vigil and culminated in the eucharistic celebration. Penance was also publicly exercised in the liturgical assembly through a process of excommunication, acts of *exomologesis* (including fasting, prayer, and almsgiving), and reconciliation with the community. It is clear that the *koinonia* experienced at the eucharistic celebration was the primary experience of Christian life.

Abbot Braso characterizes the period of the Middle Ages up through the thirteenth century as an "era of outward splendor and of lessening of solid interior piety."[10] The Western church survived the barbarian invasions and the collapse of Rome, converted the tribes of western and northern Europe, preserved in the monasteries the learning of antiquity, and infused a Christian spirit into the new social order and institutions which emerged from the ruins of the empire. The Gallican Christians had a taste for solemnity and ceremony which was merged with the chaste and sober texts of the Roman Sacramentaries imported into Charlemagne's empire. Gallican spirituality tended toward the tactile and sensual: the construction of great abbey and cathedral churches, sculpture on the stones, stained-glass windows, bells, incense, lights, and organs. The liturgy became more and more dramatic, spawning the chancel dramas of the twelfth and thirteenth centuries. Piety itself took a mimetic turn in terms of the cultivation of the imitation of Christ, especially in the ideal of poverty fostered by the religious movements of the twelfth and thirteenth centuries.

Medieval society fostered an intensely corporate spirit. Baptism, for example, made a person newly born into society a member of the political community as well as a member of the church. For the vast majority of church members baptism was as involuntary as birth. This meant that other forms of personal Christian profession were sought by many, including monastic vows, ordination to the priesthood, joining a mendicant order, or embarking on a crusade. If the individual was of little account generally in medieval society, the sacraments were nevertheless aimed at personal need. Thus baptism was the forgiveness of original sin as well as incorporation into the life of church and society. Confirmation provided a strengthening of the baptismal gift of the Holy Spirit to enable the individual to wage warfare against spiritual enemies. The private form of penance derived from the Celtic monasteries supplanted the ancient canonical public penance. The aim of penance was no longer the peace of the church, but forgiveness of personal sins. The continuing scholastic debate on the "moment of forgiveness" saw the emphasis in sacramental penance shift from the attitude of contrition (Peter Lombard) to the act of confession (Thomas Aquinas) to the declaration of absolution (Duns Scotus).[11]

The increasing individualism in piety affected a splintering of community, which was manifested in the eucharistic celebration. The altar was pushed further into the apse of the church, which was cut off from the nave by a "rood screen" designed to enable the canons to recite the prayer offices without outside interference. The sacramental elements were treated with scrupulosity, resulting in the removal of the cup from lay communicants. As a result of the heightened sense of awe attending the celebration, the canon was recited silently and the faithful did not hear it. The proliferation of priests as a result of the ordination of monks fostered the practice of saying Mass privately for special intentions. The more the Eucharist was treated as a thing rather than as an event, the less frequently the people received it. The Fourth Lateran Council had to decree that the faithful receive Holy Communion at least once a year. Only the most pious lay folk received it as often as four times a year, in spite of the fact that Masses were being celebrated almost every hour of the day!

In spite of this gradual disintegration of corporate worship, liturgy and spirituality followed the same patterns and developed in the same directions. But this development contained the seeds of the divorce between them. Liturgical formularies of the late Middle Ages tended toward sentimentality and vulgarity, especially the sequences and tropes that were inserted into almost every text of the Mass and the prayer offices.[12] The religious art of the period mirrored the piety (and perhaps contributed to it). Portrayals of Christ shifted from the early medieval triumphant Lord to the divine master and teacher of the period of the schoolmen, to the "man of sorrows" of the fifteenth century—the naked, bloody, thorn-crowned corpus hanging lifeless on the cross or lying collapsed on the lap of his sorrowing mother.[13] The multiplication of votive masses and prayer offices engendered a formalistic, indeed a mechanistic, approach toward worship. It is little wonder that people looked for spiritual life in other sources, for example, in the paraliturgical devotions that occupied them during Mass (such as the rosary or the stations of the cross) and in the numerous heretical sects which promulgated anticlerical and anti-sacramental ideas among the people (such as the Cathari, Waldenses, and Albigenses). The decay of the feudal system, the violent emergence of the nation-states, the inability of the official church to deal with its own internal decadence, all contributed to a quest for a more substantial spirituality as well as for institutional reformation. The seeds of both developments are found in the *devotio moderna*.

The Brethren of the Common Life, beginning at the end of the fourteenth century, advocated a life style based on self-examination and the cultivation of personal piety. As Braso observed, "the *devotio moderna* opened a chasm between the individual ideal of Christian perfection and the liturgical life of the church. Its characteristic note is *individualism*, and for that reason it finds itself diametrically opposed to liturgical spirituality, which is essentially ecclesiastical and communitarian."[14] The individualism of the Renaissance also provided impetus for the new attention given to personal development. It is important to remember that the major reformers of the sixteenth century were nurtured by these two movements: the *devotio moderna* and the Renaissance. Luther, for example, received his early education from the Brethren of the Common Life in Magdeburg.

The individualistic devotional prayers which came into the Mass-liturgy during the Middle Ages appealed to many of the reformers more than the ancient texts did. Thus, the semiprivate penitential sacristy prayers were turned into a devotional act for the whole congregation. Apologetic prayer formularies, such as "Lord God, the merciful, the compassionate, and the clement, here am I beginning to speak before you, I who am only dust, sinful, powerless and poor, guilty before you from my mother's womb, in exile from the moment I left her bosom, a transgressor since that time,"[15] appealed to sensibilities nurtured by the *devotio moderna*. Jungmann and Bouyer have taken delight in exposing the *Missa Illyrica,* published in 1557 by Matthias Flacius Illyricus who thought it was a Mass-text dating from the eighth century (without any mention of eucharistic presence or sacrifice), as really being a series of devotional prayers from the eleventh century said by the priest during the chants of the Mass.[16] Nevertheless, these were the kinds of prayers on which both Catholic and Protestant piety fed in the Reformation and post-Reformation periods.

The divorce between liturgy and spirituality has infected the entire Western church since the end of the Middle Ages. In the Roman church, liturgy and piety formed two distinct entities, each misunderstanding the other. People would dutifully "attend Mass" but put themselves heart and soul into devotions which have been called "popular" as a result. The prayer which formed the piety of the ancient church, morning praise and evening prayer, had been incorporated into the canonical hours of the monastic communities and changed character as a result. Matins and vespers ceased to be the communal prayer of the whole people of God and became the special obligation of monks and clergy. It is not surprising that after the Reformation we find religious orders (like the Jesuits) which for the first time gave up the choral recitation of the office in favor of the private use of the breviary.

Only in the last one hundred years has there been a gradual renewal of liturgical spirituality in the Roman church, beginning with historical-critical research into liturgical texts and traditions in the late nineteenth century and theological reflection on these sources in the early twentieth century.[17] The liturgical movement sought to combat modern individualism with a dynamic concept of the church as the body of Christ. The pastoral phase of the liturgical movement came after World War II with its emphasis on active congregational participation in the rites of the church and its urging of the reforms necessary to accomplish this.[18] The success of this movement is evident in the *Constitution on Sacred Liturgy* promulgated by the Second Vatican Council. It should be noted that the new emphasis on the *corporate* character of worship brought with it a de-emphasis on the paraliturgical devotions which had often occupied the faithful during Mass. The effort to recover a truly *liturgical* spirituality has necessitated a countering of popular piety on the part of both clergy and laity. We will see the same problems arising in the various Protestant churches when efforts have been made to implement liturgical renewal, and we will have to inquire into the root causes of this.

The quest to recapture a sense of Christian community, the emphasis on the priesthood of all believers, and the return to a more biblical and christocentric vision of worship found in the fathers are all concerns which the modern liturgical movement shares with the Reformation. The reformers removed much of the decadent late medieval underbrush of liturgical texts and practices in order to let the solid trunk of the liturgical tradition stand clear (although a few ancient limbs got chopped away with the underbrush). The rendering of liturgy in the vernacular, the inclusion of congregational songs (chants and chorales among the Lutherans, metrical psalms among the Reformed), the emphasis on biblical preaching, and the rule of no Masses without communicants were among the many reforms which aimed at recapturing the corporate character of Christian worship.[19] And while the Reformation emphasis on justification by faith alone allowed the seeds of individualism, planted in the soil of late medieval piety and Renaissance humanism, to attain a luxurious growth, liturgy served as a counterbalance. The Reformed tradition especially emphasized the corporate character of public worship by highlighting the fellowship dimension of the Lord's Supper, insisting on the celebration of baptism at the Sunday service and practicing public church discipline in the form of the ban. Lutheran liturgy, more than the Reformed, facilitated overt congregational participation through the singing of chants and hymns, even though Lutheran sacramental practice remained more personally oriented than the Reformed; that is, the reception of Holy Communion was a matter of individual decision ("the sacrament is offered to those who wish for it after they have been examined and absolved" [*Apology to the Augsburg Confession*, XXIV, 1]), baptisms were privately arranged,

THE PIETY OF WORSHIP

and private confession was practiced for a long time after the beginning of the Reformation and was even encouraged in Luther's cate-
chisms.

The deteriorization of liturgical practice in the Lutheran and Reformed churches has been blamed on Pietism, and with good reason.
But in fairness to the intentions of the pietist leaders it must be
admitted that the bureaucratic, legalistic, lifeless way in which the
cultus was maintained during the period of Protestant orthodoxy (for
example, by threats of punishment for disobedience rather than by
evangelical persuasion) justifies the pietist efforts to "convert the
outward orthodox profession into an inner, living theology of the
heart." The principal means used by the pietists to accomplish this
were small group study and prayer meetings known as *Collegia Pietatis.* Their origins may be seen in the Puritan conventicles in early
seventeenth-century England, in which the Puritans gathered for worship rather than attending the parish church where they would be
forced to use the "unscriptural" Prayer Book. In the same way, "Pietism endeavored to bring the church into the house, a living Christianity into everyday life, so that not only public worship might again
become a worship in spirit and in truth, but that the whole walk and
conversation of each one might be a sacrifice well-pleasing to God."[20]

The problem with these methods is that once they became popular,
they were opposed to the public cultus of the church. It is evident
that the "colder" experience of public worship pales in comparison
with the "warmer" experience of small group worship, especially
when *feelings* are the criterion used for judging meaningful worship.
Pietism's focus on the inner life brought to a head Protestantism's
innate distrust of externals. The result was a spirituality with little
appreciation of the values of church life. The only way Pietism could
make sense of church life was to replace the traditional liturgy of the
church with the exercises of the *collegia.* Jeremiah Ohl described
what this meant for Lutheran liturgy.

> The fixed, liturgical element was made to yield to the subjective ele-
> ment; extempore prayer was substituted for the church prayer; the
> objective church hymn gave way to hymns descriptive of the soul's
> changing conditions, experiences and feelings; the hymn-books were
> arranged according to the Order of Salvation instead of the church year;
> new melodies suited to the emotional character of the new hymns dis-
> placed the vigorous old church tunes; the sentimental aria and strains

patterned after the prevailing style in opera completely crowded out
the noble polyphonic choir music of the early masters; the order of the
Christian year was broken in the choice of texts;—in a word, what
Pietism set out to do finally resulted not in bringing about again a
proper union between the objective and the subjective, but in the
overthrow of the former and the triumph of the latter.[21]

Pietism was a pan-Protestant movement if it is viewed in the light
of various historical relationships. We have remarked on the fact that
the *collegia pietatis* were modeled after the conventicles of the English Puritans. The father of Lutheran Pietism Philip Jakob Spener
(1635–1705) read some of the writings of the Puritans in his early
years, including John Bunyan's *The Pilgrim's Progress.* He spent
time in Reformed Switzerland before earning his doctorate at
Tübingen and accepting the call to be senior pastor in Frankfurt-am-
Main. John and Charles Wesley were both influenced by the pietistic
Moravian Brethren, and John went to Germany to visit with their
leader, Count Nicholas von Zinzendorf, whose relationship with the
Lutheran church was not unlike the Wesleys' relationship with the
Anglican church. The Wesleys and their Methodist followers were in
the forefront of the evangelical revivals of the eighteenth century,
both in England and in America. These personal contacts indicate
something of the spiritual links between Puritanism, Pietism, and
Revivalism. All three placed an emphasis on the personal relationship of the individual with God rather than on doctrine, liturgy, or
polity. Adherents of these movements came to America in large numbers in the seventeenth, eighteenth, and nineteenth centuries, and
their combined influence contributed mightily to the *individualism*
which has prevaded all areas of American life and thought: in education, political theory, and social philosophy. Efforts in the Lutheran, Reformed, and Anglican communions in the mid-nineteenth
century to recover their liturgical heritages not only ran against the
prevailing piety of their members but also against the prevailing
social attitude in American culture. Roman Catholics were as much
affected by this as Protestants were. As Abbot Braso has written:

Our mentality is saturated with this individualistic view of life; and it
is very hard to abstract from anything so deeply rooted within us, and
let ourselves be penetrated with the concepts of church, community,
mystical body, which form the basis of the liturgy. The language of the
liturgy will necessarily become difficult and incomprehensible.[22]

If we are ever to recover a liturgical spirituality in this cultural context, a little more liturgical flexibility is needed than was usually displayed by liturgical reformers and renewalists in the earlier stages of liturgical recovery. Without their fanaticism, of course, we may not have come even as far as we have. But what we must do is look again at the roots of the estrangement of piety from liturgy in the late Middle Ages, analyze the kinds of practices fostered by the *devotio moderna,* and consider ways in which to amalgamate the attraction of these practices with the liturgical tradition.

Toward a Liturgical Spirituality

We have seen that the estrangement of piety from liturgy came to a head in the late Middle Ages and that reconciliation has been difficult to achieve. The overburdening of the liturgy with tropes and private prayers of a dubious quality, the quantification of celebrations, and the mechanistic way in which liturgy was done, combined with the breakdown of ecclesiastical and social structures, led to a search for other forms of devotion and contributed to the separation of public worship and personal piety from which the Western churches have not yet completely recovered.

Piety took two divergent paths in the late Middle Ages, neither of which really connected with the public liturgy of the church. One was the path of popular devotion, such as the rosary (a kind of poor man's breviary), and the Way of the Cross (a kind of poor man's pilgrimage). Carl Dehne points out that these devotions are called "popular" because: "(1) They are pitched at and practiced by ordinary Christians, and not mainly by religious professionals. (2) They appeal to a relatively large proportion of the Christian people: they attract and are spontaneously cultivated by relatively large numbers. (3) They are capable of communal celebration and are typically so celebrated: they are the prayers of structured groups of Christians and not only of individuals."[23]

These devotions are also called "paraliturgical" because they supplemented and sometimes were even substituted for the official liturgy of the church. Paraliturgical devotion of a popular sort is not unknown in Protestant practice: for example, the use of Christmas Eve candlelight services in place of the Christmas Eucharist; the use of the Easter morning sunrise service in place of the Easter Vigil; the use of popular devotional booklets for prayer at the beginning of parish council and committee meetings instead of the offices of the Liturgy of the Hours. It remains an important pastoral liturgical issue to do more than merely despise these practices. Somehow the qualities that make paraliturgical devotions "popular" should be incorporated into the official liturgy of the church.

The second path of spiritual expression at the end of the Middle Ages was the *devotio moderna.* This spiritual movement, fostered by the mendicant orders and by the Brethren of the Common Life, advocated perfection as an ideal of life eminently interior, based upon self-analysis and individual piety, and somewhat independent of the external means of grace. This movement, combined with the individualism of the Renaissance and the Reformation, opened a chasm between the personal piety and the liturgical life of the church (which must be conceived of in communitarian terms). The individual has come to be seen as the principal center of interest in spiritual life rather than the community of faith itself. Any mending of marriage between liturgy and spirituality will have to be seen in terms of a *liturgical spirituality.* As Thomas Merton has written, "The early Christian tradition and the spiritual writers of the Middle Ages knew no conflict between 'public' and 'private' prayer, or between the liturgy and contemplation. This is a modern problem. Or perhaps it would be more accurate to say it is a pseudo-problem."[24] The great master of contemplative prayer is correct here: liturgical celebration and contemplation need each other. The liturgy of the church provides a stable source and anchor for contemplation. On the other hand, "without contemplation, liturgy tends to be a mere pious show and paraliturgical prayer is plain babbling."[25]

These two types of religious expression, popular devotions and contemplation (for example, forms of meditation, spiritual exercises, and so forth) also point to two styles of worship which liturgiologists have labeled "cathedral" and "monastic."[26] These styles of prayer have emerged especially from the study of the divine office.[27] The cathedral style is characterized by repetition of formularies, a ceremonialized structure which enables people to plunge into it very easily, and simple but aggressive ritual action. The monastic style is characterized by conscious efforts at comprehension, soul-searching efforts to be honest about just where one is, and mental reflection. In short, while the cathedral style tends to be *expressive,* the monastic style tends to be *contemplative*. We should add that the cathedral style characterizes parish worship and the monastic style characterizes groups with special (and often professional) religious interests. Thus, the monastic style is not just generated by monks; it is a style into which a seminary easily falls. It can also be seen in devotions at pastors' conferences at which the clergy prefer a worship style that is informal, meditative, and void of vestments and ritual actions—the very opposite of the kind of worship which is most attractive to the ordinary layperson. Since church leaders are naturally drawn to the monastic style, the history of Christian worship has been the story of the continual efforts at monasticizing parish worship, which people have often resisted. What turns on the average layperson often turns off the average cleric.

I mention this contrast in styles because planners of worship in seminary chapels constantly raise the question of whether seminary worship should relate to the "real" worship of the church or whether it should relate to the special needs of the seminary community. It is often a disaster to try to impose one style of worship on a group which is naturally oriented toward another style. Seminary worship easily takes on an immanental, group-oriented, meditative character. Lay people appreciate the opportunity for meditation too when the environment is conducive to cultivating it (such as on a retreat, or during a weekday service, but seldom in the hustle and bustle of the parish church on Sunday morning.) In parochial situations, the consciousness of the worshiper must be invaded with aggressive ritual actions—actions that are repeated over and over again like a favorite hymn. There is a child in most of us which says, "Do it again!" The liturgy of the church is the playground of the kingdom of God in which popular things can be done again and again.

These things need not only be done in the churches. Indeed, the need for family and personal devotion as a bridge between "liturgy and life" is now widely recognized. This bridge can be crossed through the use of such popular things as lighting a baptismal candle on the anniversary of one's baptism, baking bread and buying wine for the Eucharist, and praying pared-down forms of the divine office (for example, matins, vespers, or compline) at home. Popular devotions in the home might also center around Advent wreaths, Christmas trees, palms and ashes, Easter lambs and eggs, and other things which facilitate a direct following of the church year. Scripture reading in the home can follow the cycle of readings in the Daily Lectionary (*Lutheran Book of Worship*, pp. 179ff.). Families can also increase their repertoire of hymns by singing the Sunday hymn of the day (*Lutheran Book of Worship*, pp. 929ff.) at family devotions during the week. By these means a bridge will be built between personal devotion and the public liturgy of the church.

If we are really concerned for spiritual growth in the seminary, the parish church, and the Christian home, we will have to recover the use of the daily prayer of the church. *The Lutheran Book of Worship* has provided us with offices of morning and evening prayer (matins and vespers), which blend cathedral and monastic styles. Examples of cathedral/popular features would be: the Paschal Blessing in matins; the Lucernarium, Incense, and Litany in vespers; the Psalms for daily prayer (*Lutheran Book of Worship*, p. 178) which are related to the times of celebration rather than the monastic principle of *recitatio continua*. Examples of monastic/contemplative features would be: the principle of *lectio continua* in the daily lectionary, the periods of silence after the psalms and readings, and the provision of psalter collects which provide christological/spiritual reflections on the psalms. While compline is a monastic office, in origin, its popularity springs from the fact that it also embodies qualities of the cathedral office: for example, the mutual *confiteor* at the beginning of the office and the set formularies related to the time of celebration ("at the close of the day").

Nathan Mitchell has pointed out a number of reasons why the Liturgy of the Hours can be viewed as important for spiritual growth: they are "traditional," "structured," and serve as "the sacrament of Jesus' presence as Lord of time and human history."[28] To pray within a tradition means that personal prayer can be related to the experience and hope of the community of faith. To pray within a structure means that many levels of communication can be utilized, including verbal and nonverbal, overt and covert, interpersonal and transcendent. To pray within the community's sacramental repertoire means that the pivotal times of daily life can be related to the presence of Jesus as Lord. This type of praying is not incidental to the life of the church; it is integral and constitutive. As St. John Chrysostom said, "Where there is a psalm, a prayer, a choir of prophets, a faithful band of singers, one would not be wrong in saying that there is the church."[29] If we need to learn how to pray again, this is the way the church has prayed throughout its history. Unfortunately, it has sometimes prayed the office as a legalistic obligation. But notwithstanding the legalism, the church simply does have an obligation to pray—and to pray *as church*.[30]

When the church assembles for prayer, it simply is "church" (*ecclesia*, "assembly"). God's people have gathered before their Lord, laying before him the beginning and end of their daily lives. His people do this out of a sense of devotion and love for their Lord, but also out of obedience. Prayer is established on a much firmer foundation when it is related not only to personal need (which will vary considerably from time to time) but to the apostolic injunction, "Pray without ceasing." When the church prays out of a sense of obligation it will gather for prayer when its own needs compel it to gather and even when they do not. What is at stake here is nothing less than the church's own sense of vocation and mission: to be "the first fruits of creation" (James 1:18), hallowing God's name in the world; to be the royal priesthood of the redeemed world, earnestly petitioning the coming of God's kingdom; to be the agents of God's will on earth. The sense of mission is integral to the piety of worship. It commits the church to will what it asks of God and to work for it in the world: especially daily bread, forgiveness, and reconciliation. And yet, in spite of all of its programs and activities, the church will never succeed in turning the world into the divine kingdom by its own endeavors. The adversaries of God are also abroad in the world, working their wills. Still, in the midst of every trial and tribulation, the church gathers to celebrate the victory of Christ in anticipation of that Kingdom, power, and glory which even now is setting out on the horizon of the world. The eschatological vision of the liturgy gives us a long perspective so that we are able to envision God achieving his purposes in spite of the failures, bad speculations, miscalculations, and ignorance of humanity.

The liturgy is thus able to form a disinterested and generous spirit, capable of wide horizons, which is not always comfortable with the self-serving, narrowly pragmatic interests of the marketplace (and sometimes even of religious institutions). Christians gather for prayer not because it is such a "useful" thing to do, but because they have a relationship to cultivate and deepen with their Father in heaven. In the long run it is the experience of doing something for the sheer sake of doing it (which is what devotion is), rather than for what it can accomplish, that has the formative power to transform daily life. The person who knows how to receive his daily bread with thanksgiving also knows that man does not live by bread alone.

8

the collegiality of WORSHIP

We have witnessed in recent years not only a quest for personal spiritual renewal, but also a quest for the experience of community. There are undoubtedly many sociological reasons for this. Certainly one of the major causes of social disruption has been the mobility which has characterized American society since the end of World War II. In reviewing the study of Mary Douglas in chapter 5, we have seen that the relaxing of the grip of the social group on the individual has contributed to the decline in ritualism. As she wrote, "The better defined and the more significant the social boundaries, the more bias I would expect in favor of ritual. If the social groups are weakly structured and their membership weak and fluctuating, then I would expect low value to be set on ritual performance."[1] We should not be surprised, therefore, that many of the people shopping around for a "church home" today are more disposed toward an effervescent form of religious expression than a ritualistic one. Nor should we be surprised that even some of the mainline churches have tried to attract people with more effervescent worship experiences. Such an experience minimizes the distinction between "insiders" and "outsiders."

Social mobility also suggests that the experience of community must be immediate. Migrant Americans (families of young engineers and executives as well as farm workers) do not have years in a given community to build up relationships. The experience of hospitality and acceptance must be immediate. In a study entitled *Why People Join the Church* Edward Rauff includes "the search for community" among the reasons why some people who have left the church return to it.[2] Among the characteristics that mark what he calls "magnet churches" are congregations which extend warm welcomes to outsiders and visitors.[3]

There is no doubt that the mainline churches will have to pay more attention to the preference for effervescence in religious expression in America. It is good to have congregations which extend warm welcomes to visitors. It is good to have clergy who are personally attractive and radiate love and concern. It is good to have worship experiences which "make God real," probably through the use of stirring music, pleasing surroundings, inspiring preaching, and robust sacramental celebrations. At the same time, the "ritualistic" churches will want to deny that congregations which communicate a Nordic cold shoulder are less than Spirit-filled assemblies of the body of Christ, that the ministries of clergy who are not charismatic personalities are less than effective, and that sacramental celebrations which do not look like a bath or a meal are somehow invalid. The matter of *efficacy* must be defended whenever Donatism rears its head. Donatism makes God's grace dependent on some human quality.

On the other hand, it has been said that every heresy arises because of some lack in the mainline church. The most effective way of combating Donatism is to take pains to ensure that the accusations are not well founded. Thus, some attention must be given to the quest for intimate relationships in groups where social cohesion can be quickly developed and personhood can be immediately affirmed. A large parish may even have to develop different styles of worship that may be appealing to various groups within the parish.

The Lutheran tradition has been sensitive to the need for different styles of liturgical celebration for different groups and situations. Luther provided his Latin Mass (1523) for towns and schools which had the resources to do solemn liturgies.[4] There are congregations that are capable of rich liturgical celebrations, and they should be encouraged to maintain them. There are also times and places when it is edifying to come together in large gatherings for solemn celebrations. Here one can profit from mass witness and exposure to the best that the Christian tradition has to offer. But there are also communities of Christians which cannot maintain all the riches of the tradition. Here we should remember that Luther wrote his *German Mass* (1526) "for the sake of the unlearned lay folk."[5] With its vernacular versifications and use of popular chorale tunes, the *Deutsche Messe* was, in effect, a sixteenth-century folk mass.[6] This kind of liturgical style can be implimented today by drawing on popular musical resources as a way of involving people actively in the liturgical event.

But Luther also provided a third kind of service "for those who want to be Christians in earnest." He suggested that groups "meet alone in a house somewhere to pray, to read, to baptize, to receive the sacrament, and to do other Christian works."[7] He instinctively knew (perhaps because of his monastic background) that the development of a deep spiritual life requires the kind of support structures which a small group affords. Some congregations provide this by means of weekend retreats. Other parishes offer weekday Eucharists before or after working hours which are often attended by a regular group of people, even though the service is open to the public. Some congregations provide house communions in the homes of shut-ins where members of the parish can gather together in fellowship.

One small group too long neglected is the family. Family devotions can be reestablished on a sound foundation by relating them to the prayer offices of the church. It is not beyond the capability of a Christian family to conduct vespers at dinnertime by lighting a candle, blessing God for the gift of light and creation, praying Psalm 141 or another psalm, reading a Scripture lesson, reciting the *Magnificat,* and praying an evening prayer and the Lord's Prayer. Compline would also lend itself to family devotions. In these suggestions, the preference for effervescent religious expression in our society can be channeled into traditional forms, and spirituality can be anchored in the liturgical life of the church. Conversely, these small group experiences can only enrich the church's larger and more public celebrations.

In all of these small group situations the personal orientation so much desired and needed in our society today is balanced with a sense of community by locating our common personhood in Christ in the common prayer of the church and in the sacramental celebrations. One need not resort to "touchy-feely" techniques to build community and establish interpersonal relationships. Experiences of community tend to be spontaneous, immediate, and concrete, as opposed to norm-governed, institutionalized, and abstract (which is the nature of social structure). Victor Turner suggests that "*communitas* emerges where social structure is not."[8] Or in the words of Martin Buber:

Community is being no longer side by side [and one might add, above and below] but *with* one another or a multitude of persons. And this multitude, though it moves towards one goal, yet experiences everywhere a turning to, a dynamic facing of, the others, a flowing of *I* to *Thou*. Community is where community happens.[9]

Communitas, as Turner defines it, is experienced at the margins of social structure, in a state he calls "liminality," a state betwixt and between statuses or structures. This means that *communitas* cannot exist alone; it can only exist in relationship to given social structures. Otherwise it will itself tend toward social structure. This is why *communitas* is best experienced in rites of passage, where people are removed from the social structure and are placed into marginal communities, such as on college campuses and in military boot camp, only to return to the social structure revitalized by this experience of *communitas*. Persons who have had such liminal experiences at the margins of social structure are capable of infusing new life into the social structure when they are reincorporated into it. That is why healthy societies have provided for liminal initiation processes, even though the sense of *communitas* that emerges among the initiates often expresses itself in hostility to the social structure.

This suggests two things for the life of the church. One is that it is beneficial to find ways of prolonging the liminal experience. It is characteristic of the liminal stage in rites of passage to strip away status and roles in order to emphasize undifferentiated homogenous relationships.[10] In these situations people experiencing a sense of *communitas* build close relationships with others experiencing the same thing and together they develop a sense of purpose. Something of this presumably happened in the catechumenate of the ancient church. The experience of prolonged liminality was considered so important that the monasteries developed on the heels of the demise of the catechumenate. Later on the mendicant orders emerged on the heels of the disintegration of the monastic ideal. These developments suggest that in periods of widespread dissatisfaction with institutional structures, communal expressions of anti-structure are bound to emerge. Turner calls them expressions of anti-structure not because they are unstructured, but because they emerge over against the social structure. The Puritan conventicles and Lutheran *collegia pietatis* constitute such expressions of anti-structure. Today we see prayer groups and charismatic communities emerging on the margins of congregations and denominations. Such groups could be beneficial to the whole life of the church if they were grounded in a liturgical spirituality and related to the mission of the church.

Turner's analysis suggests, secondly, that it is salutary for every Christian to experience *communitas*. This argues for the restoration of a real catechumenal experience of sufficient duration and intensity to provide for such an experience, particularly for adult converts who are being admitted into the fellowship of the church. The content of catechesis is conversion, a breaking out of status in order to acquire a new status, one that is incompatible with the former one. The *paraklesis* of Romans 12 suggests that St. Paul thought of the whole church as a community of those who have undergone transformation through the Spirit of Christ. It is an eschatological experience to receive the indwelling of the Spirit of the risen Christ. So the change of status is from "this world" to "the life of the world to come" lived here proleptically.

A church which lives "in but not of the world" will be a community always living in tension with "this world." It is on the way to the kingdom, but it is kept down to earth by the sign of the cross. It will know the suffering of humanity and bear in its body the pain of God. A community of the cross will exemplify the qualities which are the properties of liminality, or marginal experience, more than those which are associated with the status system: a sense of being in transition rather than being permanent, a desire to reach out to embrace all rather than only some, a feeling of oneness in mission rather than a toleration of "differences of opinion," a fostering of equality in the group rather than inequality, *communitas* rather than structure, and so forth.[11]

A church which bears the sign of the cross will not be concerned with property, wealth, or prestige. A church is an assembly, not an assembly hall—a congregation, not a building. To be sure, we cannot simply shed the property and buildings which the church has accumulated and constructed. But we can find ways to use our facilities that will render service to the neighborhoods in which they are located as well as shelter the congregation that worships in them. Let us remember that Christians do not need temples made with hands in order to "house" worship. Almost any kind of shelter will do for liturgy, and most of the temples we have erected do not afford the flexibility that is required either for vibrant congregational worship or for diverse group activities. The church has always had something of the nomad in its veins ("we have here no abiding city"). For nomadic life, the shelter as well as the accouterments need to be portable. If the building is nailed down, the furniture can still be movable. Even a portative pipe organ will provide adequate accompaniment for congregations of a few hundred voices. As new congregations are organized, the pressure to build should be resisted. Worship and study space can be shared or rented. One new congregation I know of is sharing space in a Franciscan priory and probably has more room at its disposal than it could afford to build. Another congregation is worshiping and studying in a shopping mall, which provides an accessibility available to few congregations.

Wealth is often associated with property. It takes money to maintain buildings and pay rising utility bills. A congregation that operates with limited facilities can afford to disregard wealth. It does not even need a lot of money to buy the accouterments for worship. Very handsome vestments, paraments, vessels, torches, crosses, candlesticks, banners, and the like, can be made by members or by persons in other congregations. Even items of furniture, such as altar and ambo, can be made by members with carpentry skills. Those with a lot of money to donate can be encouraged to put it into mission projects.

Prestige is often associated with wealth. A church that is not wealthy might be more liable to identify with the poor, the oppressed, the outcasts, and the misfits. Church leaders might find themselves standing before the bar of justice more often than sitting next to it, defending those whose rights are not easily come by.

A church without much property, wealth, or prestige is apt to have a feeling of humility, a flare for foolishness, a preference for simplicity, and a sense of the sacred. Naturally, these qualities will always have to be renewed just because it is the tendency of liminal existence to press toward status and for marginal groups to move toward the center. *Ecclesia semper reformanda*, "the church must always be reformed." The maintenance of viable experiences of *communitas* at the margins of social structure will contribute to the ongoing renewal of the church at the core of its life.

Certainly there are whole groups of Christians on the margins of the church's structure that have contributed to the renewal of liturgical life and spiritual vitality. The modern liturgical movement began with the Benedictine Revival in the nineteenth century under Dom Prosper Gueranger (1805–1875). Benedictine liturgical scholarship has been prodigious since the seventeenth century, but more recently the marginality of monasticism has been viewed as the future contribution of monks to worship and piety.[12] The *Rule of St. Benedict* continues to be important, in the words of Nathan Mitchell, "because it challenges common monastic deceptions, not because it provides contemporary monastic answers."[13] It reminds monks that they belong on the fringes of society with those "misfits" whom Merton called "the unpropertied and marginal intellectuals."[14] As monks engage in "useless prayer," their example should encourage mendicant orders such as the Franciscans and Dominicans to take their apostolic work to the fringes of society where the usual social structures lose their relevance. It is precisely in those kinds of situations that the power for change is generated.

Protestantism has not had religious groups that could so forcefully and vicariously carry on the worship and mission of the church. Yet it might just be in this context that we revisit the *collegia pietatis*. At first these groups were designed to foster the study of Scripture and the cultivation of holiness. Philip Jakob Spener also saw an interpersonal dynamic operative in such groups: "Preachers would learn to know the members of their own congregations and their weakness or growth in doctrine and piety, and a bond of confidence would be established between preachers and people which would serve the best interests of both."[15] These study and prayer groups spread quickly and became sources of division in the church, ridiculed as *ecclesiolae in ecclesia* ("little churches in the church"). In turn, some members of the groups became very critical of the official church and its ministers. Yet Pietism flourished through such groups and injected some heart into the church's worship and doctrine and provided the impetus for inner and foreign missions. August Hermann Francke and the German Pietists of the eighteenth century devoted themselves to the care of the sick, the poor, orphans, the aged, and the like as well as sending missionaries to America and other parts of the world. Once again, therefore, groups at the margins released power for change in the church as well as in society as a whole. The *collegia pietatis* offer a real challenge to the *koinonia* groups, encounter groups, and prayer groups springing up in our congregations today to concern themselves with the life and mission of the church in a direct and positive way.

Finally, let us note that there are whole congregations on the margins of the church's structures, deliberately celebrating and living the gospel on the fringes of society where failure is known more often than success. Many inner city congregations live a theology of the cross by following their Lord to defeat and rejection. It is not surprising that, in the spirit of the martyrs, the liturgical celebrations in such congregations tend to be creative and compelling. Creativity is required because such congregations minister to "misfits" who render useless many of the usual assumptions and programs of the institutional church. In such challenging and frustrating situations the public prayer of the church becomes what Thomas Merton called "the prayer of the heart . . . yearning for the simple presence of God, for a personal understanding of his word, for knowledge of his will and for capacity to hear and obey him."[16] The language of prayer and preaching tends to be simple and direct, especially in situations where many of the worshipers are less than literate. Almost as if in compensation, the actions of worship are accentuated. There is a kind of aggressive "animality" in processions, baptisms, greetings of peace, offerings, eucharistizing, eating, and drinking.

A worshiping community that finds itself in the interstices "betwixt and between" social structures is also a community which is more able to assimilate adult conversions than many status congregations where the unbridled enthusiasm of a conversion experience resulting from a crisis in life is regarded more as a threat to the status quo than something to be welcomed. For in conversion one tends to break out of accustomed roles and life styles, and to see life and its commitments and responsibilities in a new way. Persons who are going through a wrenching change of life will undoubtedly find greater receptivity in a community which itself celebrates change because its corporate life style is characterized more by transition than by fixity. It is in such congregations at the margins of church and society that catechumenal structures which facilitate the formation and initiation of adult converts are most likely to work.

There is no doubt that liturgical practices originating in marginal congregations are eventually adopted in not-so-marginal congregations. These are the contributions of marginal Christians to the rest of the body of Christ. It is in such marginal situations that we may expect to see further contributions to the liturgical and spiritual renewal and missionary impulse and social zeal of the church. For this reason we should hope that such communities will continue to flourish as sources of regenerative power for the whole church.

the practice of WORSHIP

The recognition of the communal nature of liturgical celebration has resulted in increased attention to liturgical planning in recent years. This planning concerns not only the ministers of Word and Sacrament who have sermons to prepare and sacramental rites over which to preside. It also concerns the priestly people of God who have intercessions to pray and gifts to offer. The role of the people in worship is indispensable. Even if choirs and assisting ministers take over some of the functions of the people, the people cannot be left as passive spectators. Christian worship is a participatory event. It is important for those responsible for worship planning to see that the people are encouraged and enabled to participate in worship.

Almost every matter that is important in liturgical planning concerns the people. Take the matter of *choreography*. Officiating ministers need to know where they are going when they lead public worship. But there are also times when the whole congregation is involved in movement, for example, at the greeting of peace and during the Holy Communion, and sometimes also at the entrance and offertory processions. The only way people will feel comfortable with movement in a formal situation is if they know when and where to move and what to do when they get there. This takes some forethought and planning, and maybe even a rehearsal or two until the patterns of movement become habitual. Habitual actions are not necessarily oppressive; they may also liberate and consolidate people in their relationships with one another. The more people know what is expected of them, the more they will be willing to put themselves into what is happening. One might say that the whole function of ritual pattern is to enable people to be themselves in public.

It is noteworthy that two recent books on church architecture have emphasized the primacy of persons over objects in worship. Frederic Debuyst suggested that "personalism, and the particular kind of con-

120

frontation and dialogue it inspired in the assembly, were probably the main characteristics of the celebration in that patristic era. It was also the main reason for the specific features of the basilica."[1] The dialogical character of the ancient liturgy was enhanced by the basilican architecture which located the *cathedra*, the bishop's chair, in the center of the apse, facing the congregation and surrounded by the seats of the presbyters. The bishop presided from his chair and quite often even preached while sitting in it. Between the apse and the nave was the Lord's Table. The fact that so few altars have survived from this period is easily explained because they were normally wooden and portable. During the Middle Ages the focus of the eucharistic liturgy shifted from the celebrating community to the elements. A heightened sense of awe pushed the altar into the apse, displacing the bishop's chair. The long, narrow gothic nave and the rood screen effectively excluded the people from the liturgical action. The dialogical character of worship diminished and the corporate dimension of the liturgy was dissipated by individualistic paraliturgical devotions.

The Reformation should have been able to correct this deformed piety and recapture a vital sense of the corporate nature of liturgy. But as Edward Sövik writes: "The conservative reformers were at their most conservative in matters of the environment of worship. . . . The lesson to be learned here is that architecture is a more influential factor in the life of society than most people suppose. The incompleteness of the Reformation in terms of architecture was no doubt the result of the longevity of architecture."[2] Just rearranging the furniture and changing the decorations is not enough. Environment affects the way we do things and the psychological attitude we bring to what we do. Sövik's dictum that "worship involves persons, not places" is a bit extreme in the light of what comparative religion teaches us about sacred times and places, but we cannot reform worship without taking seriously the liturgical assembly as the most important ingredient. Buildings, like the Sabbath, are made for people, not people for the buildings.

To take seriously the liturgical assembly means to relate the style of celebration to the nature of the congregation present. This is so not only in terms of the predominant age group and the socioeconomic background of the people present, but also in terms of the number of people present and the location of the worship event. One can get by with maintaining some degree of formality even in a small group meeting in a small room. But the casual intimacy that might be appropriate in a small group is inappropriate in a congregation of greater size. A large group activity in a large hall requires a certain amount of formality and a well-planned choreography.

To develop an appropriate style, therefore, does not mean relapsing into an impersonal character. But just as it is an awesome thing to come to terms with the mystery of God's presence, so it is an awesome thing to come to terms with our own presence and the presence of other people. Corporate worship requires a *dialogical character*—in terms of gesture as well as speech. It used to be customary for the celebrant to kiss the altar at the beginning of the Mass. Many Roman Catholic priests now also bow to the people. This is a gesture that recommends itself to Protestants. But as Robert Hovda writes, "There is no point in the president of the assembly bowing to you if you don't bow back."[3] There is no point in extending the arms to the people in the salutation if they do not gesture back. There is no point in inviting an acclamation from the people if they cannot make an immediate reply. How often do we have to wait for an organist to plunk a chord before we can join in acclaiming Christ at the announcement of the Gospel, or join the chorus of the heavenly host in singing the Sanctus, or even respond to the president's greeting with a simple "And also with you!" Environment can undermine the liturgy or contribute to its vibrancy; so can music and the musician.

Just as we want a worship space that is free of encumbrances so that ministers and people can move about easily, so we want a *musical style* which fosters a sense of the flow and rhythm of the liturgy. Simple plainsong settings of the dialogues and chant-texts work well when they are not encumbered with ponderous accompaniment. A greeting and response does not require organ accompaniment, and the dialogical character of the liturgy could be enhanced if we were not so dependent on accompaniment. In fact, as a general rule of thumb, dialogical versicles which are spoken should be spoken in response; and those which are sung should be sung in response. Obviously a rigid application of this rule would impoverish the liturgical celebrations of a congregation whose pastor cannot sing at all. But as an example of what can be done, it is quite gripping at the Chapel of the Resurrection at Valparaiso University when the worshiping throngs greet the announcement of the Gospel by *shouting*, rather than singing, "Glory to you, O Lord." The sung Gospel acclamations in most parishes do not come across quite as well.

Two old styles of liturgical singing which have been revived in recent years as a contribution to the dialogical character of the liturgy are antiphonal and responsorial singing. Antiphonal singing is characterized by two groups singing back and forth to one another, for example, choir and congregation. Responsorial singing would involve the congregation responding to a cantor. Several years ago Joseph Gelineau devised a method of psalm singing whereby a cantor would "line out" an antiphon (that is, a short musical refrain). The people would sing the antiphon back to the cantor, and then repeat it at the end of each verse of the psalm or canticle, which was sung by the cantor. This method of singing has tremendously aided the revival of psalmody in our churches, and it is not at all a new idea even in the Protestant tradition. In Scandinavian and Scottish churches there was the *forsinger* or *klokker* who performed a similar service before the days of mass-produced printed hymnals by "lining out" the words and phrases of the psalms and hymns. There was probably a marvelous spontaneity in this kind of congregational singing which the printed hymnals killed. It would be good to see that tradition revived because in our society it is very evident that the ability to read music has not kept apace with reading ability. Perhaps 90 percent of the members of a typical congregation cannot read music and learn only by rote. A page full of musical notation may even be intimidating to them. So antiphonal (two groups singing alternately) or responsorial (solo singing, group response) singing is an old idea whose time has come.

If the sensual arts can both contribute to and undermine dialogical liturgy, so can *words*. One cannot have monologue and dialogue at the same time. Yet so pervasive is the dialogical character of the liturgy that even monological elements such as Scripture readings, the sermon, and the eucharistic prayer are set within a dialogical framework. The responsorial psalm and the alleluia verse are responses to the first and second lessons. The sermon itself is one response to the Gospel, and the hymn of the day is a response to the sermon. In some Baptist and Pentecostal churches the congregation enters into the sermon by voicing their approval and assent to what is being said. This practice is both spontaneous and stylized, and it has the value of maintaining the sermon as an act of proclamation rather than a lecture. Current revisions of eucharistic prayers include acclamations of the people in addition to the Sanctus, such as the memorial acclamation ("Christ has died, Christ is risen, Christ will come again"), the marantha, the concluding doxology, and the Great Amen.

One element in worship which is clearly monological and which calls for some verbal restraint is the making of *announcements*. Some new Holy Communion services call for an "announcement of the day" before the first lesson or before the service begins. The purpose of this announcement is to state the theme of the service as expressed in the propers for the day. It is not another place for a sermon, much less for a lesson in exegesis. The theme should be stated in a few sentences (written out in advance if the president has a tendency to wander in discourse). The announcement of the day is not the appropriate place for parish notices. Notices of weddings, funerals, the hospitalized or ill might better be given before the intercessory prayers so that these persons can be included in the petitions. Notices of parish activities can be given at the end of the service as a way of launching the congregation into the liturgy of mission. Naturally, if attention must be called to something unusual in the service that day, it must be done before the liturgy begins. But even here it is desirable to limit the amount of explanation. For one thing, this has a tendency to put people into a defensive posture because they are being subjected to something unusual and unfamiliar. For another thing, if it is meaningful enough to do in the first place, it should convey what it means simply by doing it.

A style of *intercessory prayer* has been practiced in recent years in which the petitions are specific and the interjections by the people are welcomed. Not infrequently, however, this style of prayer has not been learned by worship leaders who insist on writing out long, verbose orations similar to the old-fashioned general prayers. As Hovda has written, "Presiding in liturgy, because it is the common deed of the entire church, requires a kind of modest prayerfulness that is heavy on awe and mystery, light on answers and recipes."[4] A rule of thumb here should be one sentence per petition, terminating in such a way that the people can voice their assent: for example, "Lord, in your mercy," with the response, "hear our prayer." When interjections of the people are invited, the intentions need not be even that formalized. It is sufficient simply to mention names or concerns aloud. When it seems that everyone has had an opportunity to add a prayer petition, the presiding minister sums up the whole intercessory prayer by a concluding formula, such as: "Into your hands, Father, we commend all for whom we pray, trusting in your mercy, through your Son, Jesus Christ our Lord."

We must avoid the temptation to turn our intercessory prayers into lectures or sermonettes. That is a ludicrous situation if we remember that our prayers are *addressed to God*! If the prayer leader thinks the value of the sermonizing is that the people are listening in, then many current models are still ludicrous because the persons who need the admonition (for example, the leaders of church and state) are not usually present. There is nothing wrong in admonishing leaders or instructing the people, but prayer is not the place for it. What, then, shall we pray for? If leaders of the congregation are involved in the hard-nosed realities of life among the members and in the wider community, they will know what to pray for. This is why deacons in the early church, who had charge of the ministry of care for others, led the prayer for the needs of the people.

We have been concerned to "curb the tongue," as Hovda says. The ultimate curbing of the tongue is *silence*. There is a need for times of reflection in the liturgy just to enable worshipers to absorb the stream of words which have been spoken and sung, prayed and proclaimed. But this is more than an opportunity for people to catch their breath; it is part of the act of worship itself. Communal periods of silence have the power to build community, just as ritual actions do. Silence can be a joint awareness of the presence of the Holy Spirit gathering the community together and opening the way for wonder at the mighty acts of God. According to Rudolf Otto, silence "is a spontaneous reaction to the feeling of the numen praesens" and "the experience of the transcendent in gracious intimate presence, the Lord's visitation of his people."[5] Silence should be incorporated into the liturgy at certain strategic places: after the invitation to pray before the prayer of the day, after the Scripture readings in the prayer offices and in the service of the Word, after the Holy Communion or before the benediction. The presiding and assisting ministers can do a lot to facilitate the use of silence by their own attitudes toward it. The length of the period of silence will depend upon the size and composition of the group. Protracted periods of silence are easier to sustain in small groups than in large groups. Needless to say silence is enhanced if there is no "mood music" in the background.

Planning a thematically unified liturgy requires the cooperation of all the worship leaders—presiding minister, assistants, organist, choir director, ushers, acolytes, altar guild, and so forth.[6] Advance planning is absolutely essential if the hymns, choir music, readings, sermon, and special ceremonies are all to fit together. While every member of the worship team has an important contribution to make, the presiding minister contributes the most to the overall unity, style, and flow of the liturgy by virtue of his or her training, knowledge, pastoral responsibility, and personal presence. Presiding in liturgy today requires more time and effort for *preparation* than has previously been the case. Sermon preparation is still a priority; but so is the preparation of prayer petitions, marking the places in the missal, gathering together the needed equipment and seeing that it is ready for use, scheduling assistants and servers, training them when necessary, and preparing a bulletin that is clear and attractive. It has been my practice in the parish to go into the chancel on Friday afternoons and pace through the whole Sunday liturgy from beginning to end, noting whether all was in readiness. If something has been overlooked, there is still time to attend to it before Sunday morning.

This kind of careful preparation has two advantages: it allows for true spontaneity and it gives worship leaders the freedom to invest themselves in the liturgy. There is a false notion of spontaneity which holds that what happens in worship should be immediately inspired by the Holy Spirit. This suggests that the Spirit does not work through the human mind, but only through human emotions. Not so! The Creator Spirit brings order out of chaos and encourages Spirit-filled people to do the same. There are some unplanned liturgical events that are such acts of chaos that the Spirit has to work overtime to make anything edifying out of them. Even charismatic worship is structured according to certain ritual patterns. Many evangelical crusades, such as those mounted by the Billy Graham Evangelistic Association, are planned in more minute detail than a Solemn High Mass. Some liturgical people find the manipulative thrust of the revival arena to be offensive, yet it has to be admitted that the revivalists have a profound understanding of human behavior. The goal of liturgical planning is not to manipulate the emotions of people, but to remove those attention-getting clumsy acts that distract people from the act of worship itself and to channel the attention of the worshipers to the proclamation. The more thorough the preparation, the more fully worship leaders and worshipers can invest themselves in the liturgical act and use it as a vehicle of devotion. This is what true spontaneity in worship is all about—being able to put oneself into the event at one's own level and according to one's own needs. The worship leader should know the liturgy like a concert artist who plays a piece of music hundreds of times but is able to bring out different nuances each time it is performed.

Our concern has been to develop a liturgical style that says that worship is a hospitable human activity, but which also conveys a sense of transcendence. These qualities are not mutually exclusive if we remember that Christian worship is incarnational and sacramental. The divine presence is mediated in, with, and under the earthly actuality. "Veiled in flesh the Godhead see!" (Charles Wesley). "Thee we adore, O hidden Savior, thee/Who in thy sacrament art pleased to be" (Thomas Aquinas). The Eucharist is the very paradigm of hospitality and transcendence because it is, phenomenologically considered, a sacred meal. Louis Bouyer wrote that "A sacred meal, by itself and without the need of anything else, actually constitutes the richest hierophany there is."[7] In the sacred meal the human community recognizes its dependence both on God and on one another. This explains why the sacred meal is the likely origin of sacrifice. As R. K. Yerkes put it:

> The word sacrifice, which means "to make a thing sacred" or "to do a sacred act," was used in Latin to describe various rites which arose from the common meal when that meal was held, not for the ordinary purpose of satisfying hunger, but for the sake of entering into union with the mysterious Power or powers which men felt within them and about them as life itself, and which they recognized in all their environments as both menacing and strengthening the life which they loved and to which they longed to cling.[8]

It is instructive to remember that the Jewish Passover meal is such a communion sacrifice, and that it provides the background for the Christian eucharistic meal as both communion and thank offering, as both the most intimate form of fellowship and the highest act of worship.

In the planning and practice of worship we cannot ignore the power of *natural symbols*. They serve as a basis of correlation between cult and culture. If the Lord's Supper is a *meal*, then all the dymanics of a meal cluster around it. Schmemann calls the meal "the last 'natural sacrament' of family and friendship, of life that is more than 'eating' and 'drinking.'"[9] Eating can be strictly utilitarian when it involves no more than maintaining bodily functions. We can fulfill our basic animal needs by pouring a bowl of packaged cereal in the morning, opening a can of soup at lunch, and throwing together some Hamburger Helper at dinner. This is what we sometimes do when we are alone or in a hurry. But we do more than that when we are with family or friends. We take time to socialize with them at the table; we *dine*. What does such dining mean? It may mean any number of things: the celebration of the birth of a child, a job promotion, the reunion of old friendships, a significant anniversary, and the like. Dining for such purposes *transcends* the mere act of eating and drinking. And when we can afford it, we would like a tablecloth, lighted candles, an attentive waiter, and live music in the background. We would like to dine graciously. I would suggest that this is the up-to-date counterpart of the primitive sacred meal, and it says something about the care that should be devoted to the central liturgical act of the church.

There have been many critics in recent years who have said that we have failed to incorporate living symbols into the liturgy. There may be some truth to that. But I think some of those symbols are more readily available than we have thought. We do not need to manufacture symbols to relate liturgy to everyday life. I agree with Ralph Keifer that what we need to do is to exploit the symbolic vocabulary that has been there all along in the liturgy. He has suggested that "the primordial Christian liturgical symbols are really reducible to four: assembling, bathing, caressing, and dining." In demonstrating the social, relational, nonutilitarian, transcendent character of each of these symbols, he points out that "not all gathering is assembling, not all washing is bathing, not all touching is caressing, and not all eating is dining."[10]

We may gather like a bunch of commuters waiting for a train, or we may assemble like a family for a reunion. We may wash in order to clean ourselves, or we may bathe in order to recreate. We may shake someone's hand in order to fulfill a social convention, or we may caress in order to seal a relationship of love. We may eat just to receive biological nourishment, or we may dine in order to celebrate something important in our lives. Just so, there are worship services where people gather like herds and services where they come together to be with one another in the presence of the Lord. There are baptisms performed in relative privacy to do what is minimally necessary to signify the forgiveness of sin. But there are also baptisms that publicly celebrate the establishment of a new relationship with God and his people. There are trickles of water, dabs of oil, and pats on the head that effectively disengage the body from worship even at the very moment of incorporation into Christian worship. But there are also robust gestures that give the body full play and let people know they are really included in what is going on. There are Holy Communion services where people line up at the counter row by row to eat a paper-thin wafer and drink a thimble of wine. But there are also Holy Communion services where broken pieces of bread and shared goblets of wine bespeak a feast and evoke the fellowship of the eschatological banquet. In sum, there are liturgies that foster collectivism or individualism, keep relationships formal and distant, and accomplish what is rubrically obligatory. But there are also liturgies which form community, foster relationships, and allow people to enjoy the act of worship. One style of worship is not necessarily less genuine than the other, depending upon "the inward thoughts of the heart." But one style allows people to express themselves in a public situation while the other one minimizes such self-expression. The one style says in a direct way what the church is all about, and the other style may leave some folks guessing or communicate answers which are less than theologically or strategically desirable.

Such considerations suggest that worship planners need to know what is *really* going on in the liturgy. This might mean suspending the analysis of what symbols mean and asking instead what effect they might have on people. It might mean employing the insights and methods of communications theory in order to develop greater sensitivity to the thousand-and-one potential distractions to the liturgical celebration.[11] Yet in spite of the banging of radiator pipes; an atmosphere that is either too hot or too cold for comfort; the smell of frying fish oozing up from the church basement; electrical fixtures that cast either too much light or not enough; lectors whose rendition of the Word of God is unaudible; choirs whose dissonance is unintentional; organists whose playing is too self-consciously dramatic; preachers who confuse their own offensiveness with the offense of the gospel; and Holy Communion assistants who look like they need a lot of help; people keep returning. In the last analysis, what is really going on is the work of the Holy Spirit. We do not always know what we are doing, but the Spirit helps us in our weakness. For we, the people of God, always seem to muddle through in ways appropriate to our own time and place. This is undoubtedly because we are, for better or for worse, a part of our own time and place and in the Spirit that enables the worship of faltering earthly pilgrims to be joined with the worship of all the company of heaven. If what results for us does not quite seem to be heaven on earth, there is certainly enough eschatological charge in it to transform the things of earth into vessels of the holy.

NOTES

INTRODUCTION

1. On the question of indigenization see J. R. Chandran and W. Q. Lash, eds., *Christian Worship in India* (Bangalore, 1961) and H. Sawyerr, *Creative Evangelism: Towards a New Christian Encounter with Africa* (London: Lutterworth Press, 1968), especially chapter 5 on "A Fresh Liturgical Approach."

2. Among classic introductions are W. K. Lowther Clark and Charles Harris, *Liturgy and Worship* (London: SPCK, 1932); Josef A. Jungmann, *Public Worship: A Survey*, trans. Clifford Howell (Collegeville, Minn.: Liturgical Press, 1957); and Luther D. Reed, *The Lutheran Liturgy*, 2d ed. (Philadelphia: Fortress Press, 1959). Of more recent vintage are Cheslyn Jones, Geoffrey Wainwright, and Edward Yarnold, eds., *The Study of Liturgy* (New York and London: Oxford University Press, 1978); Philip Pfatteicher and Carlos Messerli, *Manual on the Liturgy: Lutheran Book of Worship* (Minneapolis: Augsburg Publishing House, 1979); Charles Price and Louis Weil, *Liturgy for Living* (New York: Seabury Press, 1979); and James F. White, *Introduction to Christian Worship* (Nashville: Abingdon Press, 1980).

3. One of the best books on pastoral liturgics in recent years is Paul Waitman Hoon, *The Integrity of Worship* (Nashville: Abingdon Press, 1971). On the relationship between cult and culture see also Jean-Jacques von Allmen, *Worship: Its Theology and Practice*, trans. Harold Knight and W. Fletcher Fleet (London: Lutterworth Press, 1965).

4. Margaret Mead, cited in Ruth Benedict, *Patterns of Culture* (Boston: Houghton Mifflin, 1934), p. vii. John Beattie, *Other Cultures* (New York: Free Press, 1964), likewise defines culture as "the whole range of human activities which are learned and not instinctive, and which are transmitted from generation to generation through various learning processes" (p. 20).

CHAPTER 1

1. Morton T. Kelsey, *Myth, History, and Faith: The Remythologizing of Christianity* (Ramsey, N.J.: Paulist Press, 1974), p. 2.

2. C. G. Jung, *Psychology and Religion: East and West*, Collected Works 11 (New York: Pantheon Books, 1958), p. 334.

3. See Mary Douglas, *Natural Symbols: Explorations in Cosmology* (New York: Pantheon Books, 1973), pp. 19ff.

4. Cited in Roland A. Delattre, "Ritual Resourcefulness and Cultural Pluralism," *Soundings* 41 (1978): 286.

5. Margaret Mead, "Ritual Expression of the Cosmic Sense," *Worship* 40 (1966): 71.

6. Aidan Kavanagh, "The Theology of Easter: Themes in Cultic Data," *Worship* 42 (1968): 198.

7. Mircea Eliade, *Patterns in Comparative Religion* (Cleveland: World Publishing, Meridian Books, 1963), p. 32.

8. Naham N. Glatzer, ed., *The Passover Haggadah: Including Readings on the Holocaust: With English Translation, Introduction, and Commentary* (New York: Schocken Books, 1953, 1969), p. 51.

9. Josef Pieper, *In Tune with the World: A Theory of Festivity* (Chicago: Franciscan Herald Press, 1973), p. 30.

10. Aidan Kavanagh, "The Role of Ritual in Personal Development," in *The Roots of Ritual,* ed. James Shaughnessy (Grand Rapids: Wm. B. Eerdmans, 1973), p. 149.

11. Louis Bouyer, *Rite and Man: Natural Sacredness and Christian Sacraments* (Notre Dame, Ind.: University of Notre Dame Press, 1963), p. 64.

12. See Mircea Eliade, *The Sacred and the Profane* (New York: Harper Torchbooks, 1961).

13. Arnold Van Gennep, *The Rites of Passage* (Chicago: University of Chicago Press, 1960), p. 2.

14. Victor Turner, *The Forest of Symbols* (Ithaca, N.Y.: Cornell University Press, 1967), p. 96.

15. Van Gennep, *Rites of Passage,* p. 29.

16. See R. K. Yerkes, *Sacrifice in Greek and Roman Religion and Early Judaism* (London: A & C Black, 1953).

17. See the chapter "Anthropology and Liturgy" in Gwen Kennedy Neville and John H. Westerhoff III, *Learning Through Liturgy* (New York: Seabury Press, 1978), pp. 71ff.

CHAPTER 2

1. See Jaroslav Pelikan, *Obedient Rebels: Catholic Substance and Protestant Principle in Luther's Reformation* (New York: Harper & Row, 1964), p. 78.

2. Martin Luther, "An Order of Mass and Communion for the Church at Wittenberg," *Luther's Works,* 55 vols. (Philadelphia: Fortress Press; St. Louis: Concordia Publishing House, 1955–), 53:19. Hereafter referred to as *LW.*

3. Ibid., p. 82.

4. See the "Brief Confession Concerning the Holy Sacrament, 1544," in *LW* 38: 313–19.

5. *The Book of Concord*, trans. and ed. Theodore G. Tappert (Philadelphia: Fortress Press, 1959), p. 36.

6. Clifford W. Dugmore, *The Influence of the Synagogue Upon the Divine Office* (London: Faith Press, 1964), pp. 102ff.

7. Joachim Jeremias, *The Eucharistic Words of Jesus*, trans. Norman Perrin (Philadelphia: Fortress Press, 1977), argues convincingly in favor of the Passover setting of the Last Supper.

8. *The Mishnah*, ed. and trans. Herbert Danby (New York: Oxford University Press, 1933), pp. 2ff.

9. See David Hedegard, *Seder Rav Amran Gaon*, Part I (Lund, 1951).

10. Mishnah, *Berakoth* 6.1, and Tosefta 4.8.

11. See Arthur Vööbus, *Liturgical Traditions in the Didache* (Stockholm: Estonian Theological Society in Exile, 1968), pp. 16aff.

12. Texts in Louis Finkelstein, "The Birkat ha-Mazon," *Jewish Quarterly Review* 19 (1928–29): 215–16.

13. For texts see *Prayers of the Eucharist*, ed. R. C. D. Jasper and G. J. Cuming (New York: Oxford University Press, 1980), pp. 21ff., 26ff.

14. Jean Danielou, *The Theology of Jewish Christianity*, trans. John A. Baker (Chicago: Henry Regnery, 1964), pp. 156–57.

15. See Louis Bouyer, *Eucharist*, trans. Charles U. Quinn (Notre Dame, Ind.: University of Notre Dame Press, 1968). The most promising research into the development of the anaphora is Louis Ligier, "The Origins of the Eucharistic Prayer: From Last Supper to the Eucharist," *Studia Liturgica* 9 (1973): 111–85. See also the conclusions drawn from Ligier's work by Thomas J. Talley, "From Berakah to Eucharistein: A Reopening Question," *Worship* 50 (1976): 138–58.

16. Gregory Dix, *The Shape of the Liturgy* (London: Dacre Press, 1945), pp. 48ff.

17. For a general survey of the Byzantine Liturgy see Juan Mateos, "The Evolution of the Byzantine Liturgy," *John XXIII Lectures*, Vol. 1 (New York: Fordham University Press, 1966), pp. 76–112; and Robert F. Taft, "The Great Entrance," in *Orientalia Christiana Analecta* 200 (Rome, 1975). The best study of the Roman liturgy is Josef A. Jungmann, *The Mass of the Roman Rite*, 2 vols., trans. F. Brunner (New York: Denziger Brothers, 1951, 1955).

18. For texts of the liturgies of the major Protestant traditions see Bard Thompson, *Liturgies of the Western Church* (Philadelphia: Fortress Press, 1980).

19. See Doug Adams, *Meeting House to Camp Meeting: Toward a History of American Free Church Worship from 1620 to 1835* (Austin, Tex.: Sharing Company, 1981).

20. See T. W. Manson, "Entry into Membership of the Early Church," *Journal of Theological Studies* 48 (1947): 25–33.

21. On the origins of baptismal anointing see Leonel L. Mitchell, *Baptismal Anointing* (London: SPCK, 1966), pp. 1–29.

22. See *The Treatise on The Apostolic Tradition of St. Hippolytus of Rome*, ed. and trans. Gregory Dix (London: SPCK, 1968), pp. 23–24.

23. See Edward J. Yarnold, *The Awe-Inspiring Rites of Initiation: Baptismal Homilies of the Fourth Century* (New York: St. Paul Publications, 1972).

24. The most comprehensive study of the disintegration of Christian initiation in the medieval West is J. D. C. Fisher, *Christian Initiation: Baptism in the Medieval West* (London: SPCK, 1965).

25. J. D. C. Fisher, *Christian Initiation: The Reformation Period* (London: SPCK, 1970), pp. 9ff., places in parallel columns the Order of Baptism in the Magdeburg Agenda (1497) and Luther's Order of Baptism (1523).

26. See Nathan Mitchell, "Dissolution of the Rite of Christian Initiation," in *Made, Not Born: New Perspectives on Christian Initiation and the Catechumenate*, ed. The Murphy Center for Liturgical Research (Notre Dame, Ind.: University of Notre Dame Press, 1976), pp. 50–82, for an especially clear presentation on medieval interpretations of confirmation.

27. See Fisher, *Christian Initiation*, pp. 102–3.

28. See Arthur Repp, *Confirmation in the Lutheran Church* (St. Louis: Concordia Publishing House, 1964), chapters 1–2.

29. See A. M. Roguet, *Christ Acts Through Sacraments*, trans. Carisbrooke Dominicans (Collegeville, Minn.: Liturgical Press, 1954).

30. See *The Rites of the Catholic Church as Revised by the Second Vatican Ecumenical Council* (New York: Pueblo Publishing Co., 1976), pp. 3ff. The most thorough and provocative commentary on the Rites of Christian Initiation of Adults is Aidan Kavanagh, *The Shape of Baptism: The Rite of Christian Initiation* (New York: Pueblo Publishing Co., 1978). For a further assessment of the cultural situation which is calling for a radical reevaluation of baptismal policy see Ralph A. Keifer, "Christian Initiation: The State of the Question," in *Made, Not Born*, ed. Murphy Center, pp. 138–151.

31. *Lutheran Book of Worship*, Pew Edition (Minneapolis: Augsburg Publishing House; Philadelphia: Board of Publication of the Lutheran Church in America, 1978), pp. 121–24. See also Frank C. Senn, "The Shape and Content of Christian Initiation: An Exposition of the New Lutheran Liturgy of Holy Baptism," *Dialog* 14 (1975): 97–107.

32. *Lutheran Book of Worship*, pp. 198–201. See Frank C. Senn, "An End for Confirmation?" *Currents in Theology and Mission* 3 (1976): 45–52.

33. On the question of infant communion see J. M. M. Dalby, "The End of Infant Communion," *Church Quarterly Review* 167 (1966): 59–71; Charles Crawford, "Infant Communion: Past Tradition and Present Practices," *Theological Studies* 31 (1970): 523–36; Eugene L. Brand, "Baptism and Communion of Infants: A Lutheran View," *Worship* 50 (1976): 29–43; David L. Pearcy, "Infant Communion," *Currents in Theology and Mission* 7 (1980): 43–47, 166–70; 8 (1981): 162–65; *And Do Not Hinder Them: An ecumenical plea for the admission of children to the Eucharist*, ed. by Geiko Müller-Fahrenholz. Faith and Order Paper No. 109 (Geneva: World Council of Churches, 1982).

34. See Erik Erikson, "Ontegeny of Ritualization in Man," *Philosophical Transactions of the Royal Society of London*, Series B, no. 772, vol. 251 (1966), pp. 337–50. See also Aidan Kavanagh, "The Role of Ritual in Personal Development," in *The Roots of Ritual*, ed. James Shaughnessy (Grand Rapids: Wm. B. Eerdmans, 1973), pp. 145–60.

CHAPTER 3

1. See H. Richard Niebuhr, *Christ and Culture* (New York: Harper & Row, 1951), pp. 45ff. See also Charles Norris Cochrane, *Christianity and Classical Culture* (New York: Oxford University Press, 1940).

2. Alexander Schmemann, *Introduction to Liturgical Theology* (London: Faith Press, 1966), p. 88.

3. Josef A. Jungmann, *The Early Liturgy to the Time of Gregory the Great*, trans. Francis A. Brunner (Notre Dame, Ind.: University of Notre Dame Press, 1959), pp. 145ff.

4. See Theodore Klauser, *A Short History of the Western Liturgy*, trans. John Halliburton (New York: Oxford University Press, 1969), pp. 54ff.

5. Edmund Bishop, "The Genius of the Roman Rite," in *Liturgica Historica* (New York: Oxford University Press, 1918), p. 19.

6. See the characterization of the various historical periods within the Western Middle Ages in R. W. Southern, *Western Society and the Church in the Middle Ages*, Pelican History of the Church 2 (Baltimore: Penguin Books, 1970), pp. 24ff.

7. Nathan Mitchell, O.S.B., *Cult and Controversy: The Worship of the Eucharist Outside Mass* (New York: Pueblo Publishing Co., 1982), pp. 367ff.

8. See Gabriel Braso, O.S.B., *Liturgy and Spirituality*, trans. Leonard J. Doyle (Collegeville, Minn.: Liturgical Press, 1971), pp. 39ff.

9. See Luther D. Reed, *The Lutheran Liturgy*, 2d ed. (Philadelphia: Fortress Press, 1959), pp. 69ff.

10. See John P. Dolan, *History of the Reformation* (New York: Desclee, 1965), pp. 139ff.

11. See George William Outram Addleshaw and Frederick Etchells, *The Architectural Setting of Anglican Worship* (London: Faber & Faber, 1948), pp. 22ff.

12. Quoted in Jeremiah F. Ohl, "The Liturgical Deteriorization of the Seventeenth and Eighteenth Centuries," *Memoirs of the Lutheran Liturgical Association* 4 (1906): 77.

13. See George Feder, "Decline and Restoration," in *Protestant Church Music*, ed. Fredrich Blume (New York: W. W. Norton & Co., 1974), pp. 319ff.

14. See Ernst Koenker, *The Liturgical Renaissance in the Roman Catholic Church* (St. Louis, Concordia Publishing House, 1966), pp. 9ff.

15. James F. White, *Christian Worship in Transition* (Nashville: Abingdon Press, 1976), pp. 76ff.

16. Ibid., pp. 131ff.
17. Kenneth Smits, "Liturgical Reform in Cultural Perspective," *Worship* 50 (1976): 98ff.
18. See E. Franklin Frazier, *The Negro Church in America* (New York: Schocken Books, 1964).
19. See Charles G. Adams, "Some Aspects of Black Worship," *Journal of Church Music* 15 (February 1973): 2–9, 16.
20. See Roberto Escamilla, "Fiesta Worship," *The Interpreter* (June 1976).
21. See Miles Mark Fisher, *Negro Slave Songs in the United States*, rev. ed. (Ithaca, N.Y.: Cornell University Press, 1968); and Christa Dixon, *Negro Spirituals* (Philadelphia: Fortress Press, 1976).
22. Vigilio P. Elizondo, *Christianity and Culture: An Introduction to Pastoral Theology and Ministry for the Bicultural Community* (Huntington, Ind.: Our Sunday Visitor, n.d.), p. 172.
23. Ricardo Ramirez, "Liturgy from the Mexican American Perspective," *Worship* 51 (July 1977): 295.

CHAPTER 4

1. Paul Waitman Hoon, *The Integrity of Worship* (Nashville: Abingdon Press, 1971), p. 215.
2. Daniel B. Stevick, "Renewing the Language of Worship," in *Worship: Good News in Action*, ed. Mandus Egge (Minneapolis: Augsburg Publishing House, 1973), pp. 111–26.
3. Marshall McLuhan, *Understanding Media: The Extensions of Man* (New York: New American Library, Signet Books, 1964), p. 36.
4. Louis Bouyer, *Rite and Man: Natural Sacredness and Christian Sacraments* (Notre Dame, Ind.: University of Notre Dame Press, 1963), p. 61.
5. *The First and Second Prayer Books of King Edward VI*, Everyman's Library (London: Dent, 1910), p. 4.
6. See Theodor Klauser, *A Short History of the Western Liturgy*, Eng. trans. John Halliburton (Oxford University Press, 1979), pp. 117ff.
7. *LW* 40: 141.
8. See Luther D. Reed, *The Lutheran Liturgy*, 2d ed. (Philadelphia: Fortress Press, 1959), pp. 88ff.
9. See Josef A. Jungmann, *The Mass of the Roman Rite*, vol. 1, trans. F. Brunner (New York: Denziger Brothers, 1951, 1955), pp. 104f. The same process can be seen in the development of the breviary in the thirteenth century in order to put into a single volume for itinerant friars all that was needed for the daily prayer offices. This contributed to the solo recitation of the divine office.
10. Ibid., vol. 2, p. 118.
11. See Philip Pfatteicher and Carlos R. Messerli, *Manual on the Liturgy:*

Lutheran Book of Worship (Minneapolis: Augsburg Publishing House, 1979), pp. 195–96, 211.

12. Hoon, *Integrity of Worship*, pp. 63–64.

13. Jaroslav Pelikan, *Fools for Christ* (Philadelphia: Muhlenberg Press, 1955), p. 152.

14. Joseph Gelineau, S.J., *Voices and Instruments in Christian Worship*, trans. Clifford Howell, S.J. (Collegeville, Minn.: Liturgical Press, 1963), p. 216.

15. Joseph Sittler, *The Ecology of Faith* (Philadelphia: Muhlenberg Press, 1961), p. 96.

CHAPTER 5

1. Quoted in Clement J. McNaspy, S.J., *Our Changing Liturgy* (Garden City, N.J.: Doubleday Image Books, 1967), pp. 13–14.

2. Mary Douglas, *Natural Symbols: Explorations in Cosmology* (New York: Pantheon Books, 1973), p. 20.

3. Margaret Mead, "Ritual and Social Crisis," in *The Roots of Ritual*, ed. James Shaughnessy (Grand Rapids: Wm. B. Eerdmans, 1973), p. 97.

4. Melvin Maddocks, "Rituals—The Revolt Against the Fixed Smile," *Time* (October 12, 1970): 42.

5. Douglas, *Natural Symbols*, pp. 77ff.

6. Ibid., p. 25.

7. Basil Bernstein, "A Socio-Linguistic Approach to Social Learning," in *Penguin Survey of the Social Sciences*, ed. J. Gould (London: Penguin Books, 1965).

8. Douglas, *Natural Symbols*, p. 57.

9. Ibid., pp. 72–73.

10. Ibid., p. 74.

11. Ibid., pp. 93ff.

12. Ibid., pp. 103–4.

13. Ibid., p. 32.

14. J. A. T. Robinson, *The Body: A Study in Pauline Theology* (London: SCM Press, 1952), p. 14.

15. Paul Waitman Hoon, *The Integrity of Worship* (Nashville: Abingdon Press, 1971), pp. 316ff.

16. Margaret Mead, "Ritual Expression of the Cosmic Sense," *Worship* 40 (1966): 71.

17. Alexander Schemann, *For the Life of the World* (Crestwood, N.Y.: St. Vladimir's Seminary Press, 1974), p. 27.

18. Hoon, *Integrity of Worship*, p. 324. One of the most powerful statements of the ethical implications of liturgical celebration was made by Bishop J. A. T. Robinson, *Liturgy Coming to Life* (Philadelphia: Westminster Press, 1960), who spoke of Holy Communion as "social dynamite" (pp. 25–26). The Catholic moral theologian Bernard Häring, *The Sacra-*

ments in a Secular Age: A Vision in Depth on Sacramentality and Its Impact on Moral Life (Slough: St. Paul Publications, 1976), regards sacraments as signs to sharpen our vision of the divine presence in the world and as gifts which enable us to conform our will and action to that of God's will in Christ.

CHAPTER 6

1. See the discussion in Geoffrey Wainwright, Doxology: A Systematic Theology (New York: Oxford University Press, 1980), pp. 218–83.

2. See Josef A. Jungmann, The Early Liturgy to the Time of Gregory the Great, trans. Francis A. Brunner (Notre Dame, Ind.: University of Notre Dame Press, 1959), chapter 15.

3. Ibid., pp. 115ff.

4. Wainwright, Doxology, pp. 16ff.

5. Alexander Schmemann, "Worship in a Secular Age," appended to For the Life of the World (Crestwood, N.J.: St. Vladimir's Seminary Press, 1974), p. 118.

6. James F. White, The Worldliness of Worship (New York: Oxford University Press, 1967), p. 82.

7. Schmemann, "Worship in a Secular Age," p. 125.

8. C. G. Jung, Psychological Types (London: Routledge & Kegan Paul, 1949), p. 601.

9. Peter Brunner, Worship in the Name of Jesus, trans. Martin H. Bertram (St. Louis: Concordia Publishing House, 1968), pp. 126ff., 197ff.

10. Apology to the Augsburg Confession, Article XXIV in The Book of Concord, trans. and ed. Theodore G. Tappert (Philadelphia: Fortress Press, 1959), p. 36.

11. See "An Order of Mass and Communion for the Church at Wittenberg," LW 53:25ff.

12. The First and Second Prayer Books of King Edward VI, Everyman's Library (London: Dent, 1910), p. 222.

13. Brunner, Worship in Name of Jesus, p. 207. See also Geoffrey Wainwright, Eucharist and Eschatology (New York: Oxford University Press, 1971, 1981), who develops the meanings of the Eucharist as the ante-past of heaven, the Parousia of Christ, and the first fruits of the kingdom. On the relationship between the Eucharist and the Lord's Day see Willy Rordorf, Sunday, trans. A. A. K. Graham (Philadelphia: Westminster Press, 1968), pp. 274ff.

14. Evelyn Underhill, Worship (New York: Harper Torchbooks, 1936), p. 3.

15. Augustine The City of God 10.6 (trans. Henry Betterson, ed. David Knowles [Baltimore: Penguin Books, 1972], p. 380).

16. See Robert J. Ledogar, "The Eucharistic Prayer and the Gifts over which it is Spoken," Worship 41 (1968): 578–96.

17. *Lutheran Book of Worship*, Ministers Edition (Minneapolis: Augsburg Publishing House; Philadelphia: Board of Publication, Lutheran Church in America, 1978), p. 226.

18. *Byzantine Daily Worship*, ed. the Most Reverend Joseph Raya and Baron Jose de Vinck (Allendale, N.J.: Alleluia Press, 1969), pp. 284–85.

19. Josef A. Jungmann, *The Mass of the Roman Rite*, vol. 2, trans. F. Brunner (New York: Denziger Brothers, 1951, 1955), p. 233.

20. See John Jay Hughes, "Eucharistic Sacrifice: Transcending the Reformation Deadlock," *Worship* 43 (1969): 532–44.

21. Leslie A. White, *The Evolution of Culture* (New York: McGraw-Hill, 1959), developed the controversial thesis that technology is the basis of culture, even of religious culture.

22. Wainwright, *Doxology*, pp. 388ff.

23. Brian Spinks, "Christian Worship or Cultural Incantation?" *Studia Liturgica* 12 (1977): 1–19.

24. H. Richard Niebuhr, *Christ and Culture* (New York: Harper & Row, 1951), pp. 128ff.

25. Ibid., pp. 170ff.

26. Lutheran theologians in the twentieth century have been somewhat wary of the two kingdom ethic. For a discussion of the issues in the debate see Hans Schwartz, "Luther's Doctrine of the Two Kingdoms—Help or Hindrance in Social Change?" *Lutheran Quarterly* 27 (1975): 59–79.

27. Wainwright, *Doxology*, p. 394.

28. Niebuhr, *Christ and Culture*, pp. 218ff.

29. Nicholas Berdyaev, *Slavery and Freedom*, trans. R. M. French (New York: Charles Scribner's Sons, 1944), p. 18. Berdyaev's "mystical anarchism" is very interesting as an approach toward living "in, but not of the world." See Frank C. Senn, "Berdyaev, Orthodoxy, and the Theology of Hope," *Journal of Ecumenical Studies* 7 (1970): 455–75.

30. Nicholas Berdyaev, *The Destiny of Man*, trans. Natalie Duddington (New York: Harper & Row, 1960), distinguished between the ethics of law, the ethics of redemption, and the ethics of creativeness as he moved from general principles of philosophical ethics, through the radical ethics of the gospel, to the interim ethics of those who live in this world oriented toward the kingdom of God.

CHAPTER 7

1. See Ralph A. Keifer, "How About Devotion at Mass?" *Living Worship* 12, no. 3 (March 1976).

2. Gabriel Braso, O.S.B., *Liturgy and Spirituality*, trans. Leonard J. Doyle (Collegeville, Minn.: Liturgical Press, 1971), p. 28.

3. *Romans* 4:1 in *Early Christian Fathers*, vol. I of Library of Christian Classics, trans. and ed. Cyril C. Richardson with Eugene R. Fairweather,

Edward Rochie Hardy, and Massey Hamilton Shepherd (Philadelphia: West-minster Press, 1953), p. 105.

4. *Ephesians* 10:3 in *Early Christian Fathers*, p. 91.

5. *Philadelphians* 4 in *Early Christian Fathers*, p. 109.

6. *Martyrdom of Polycarp* 14:2 in *Early Christian Fathers*, p. 154.

7. *Martyrdom of Polycarp* 15:2 in *Early Christian Fathers*, p. 155.

8. Thus Tertullian *Concerning Baptism* 16.2; Hippolytus *The Apostolic Tradition*, Part II, 19.2; Augustine *The City of God* 8.7.

9. Louis Bouyer, *A History of Christian Spirituality*, vol. I: *The Spirituality of the New Testament and the Fathers*, Eng. trans. (New York: Desclee, 1960), p. 210.

10. Braso, *Liturgy and Spirituality*, p. 35.

11. See the symposium on penance in *Resonance* 2 (1966). See also Nathan Mitchell, O.S.B., ed., *The Rites of Penance: Commentaries*, vol. III: *Background and Directions* (Washington, D.C.: Liturgical Conference, 1978).

12. Braso, *Liturgy and Spirituality*, pp. 39ff.

13. See Josef A. Jungmann, *Pastoral Liturgy*, Eng. trans. (New York: Herder & Herder, 1962).

14. Braso, *Liturgy and Spirituality*, p. 43.

15. Cited in Louis Bouyer, *Eucharist*, trans. Charles U. Quinn (Notre Dame, Ind.: University of Notre Dame Press, 1968), p. 378.

16. Ibid., p. 379.

17. See Louis Bouyer, *Liturgical Piety* (Notre Dame, Ind.: University of Notre Dame Press, 1956), chapters 1–5.

18. See Ernest B. Koenker, *The Liturgical Renaissance in the Roman Catholic Church* (St. Louis: Concordia Publishing House, 1966), chapters 3–6.

19. See Luther D. Reed, *The Lutheran Liturgy*, 2d ed. (Philadelphia: Fortress Press, 1959), pp. 140ff.

20. Jeremiah F. Ohl, "The Liturgical Deteriorization of the Seventeenth and Eighteenth Centuries," Memoirs of the Lutheran Liturgical Association 4 (1906): 69.

21. Ibid., p. 70.

22. Braso, *Liturgy and Spirituality*, p xiv.

23. Carl Dehne, S.J., "Roman Catholic Popular Devotions," in *Christians at Prayer*, ed. John Gallen, S.J. (Notre Dame, Ind.: University of Notre Dame Press, 1976), p. 86.

24. Thomas Merton, *Contemplative Prayer* (Garden City, N.Y.: Double-day Image Books, 1969), p. 46.

25. Ibid., p. 114.

26. See William G. Storey, "The Liturgy of the Hours: Cathedral versus Monastery," in *Christians at Prayer*, ed. Gallen, pp. 61–82.

27. See W. Jardine Grisbrooke, "The Formative Period: Cathedral and Monastic Offices," in *The Study of Liturgy*, ed. Cheslyn Jones, Geoffrey

Wainwright, and Edward Yarnold (New York and London: Oxford University Press, 1978), pp. 358–69.

28. Nathan Mitchell, O.S.B., "Useless Prayer," in *Christians at Prayer,* ed. Gallen, pp. 21–23.

29. *Expositio in Psalmum 41,* cited in *ibid.,* p. 23.

30. See J.-J. von Allmen, "The Theological Meaning of Common Prayer," *Studia Liturgica* 10 (1974): 125–36.

CHAPTER 8

1. Mary Douglas, *Natural Symbols: Explorations in Cosmology* (New York: Pantheon Books, 1973), pp. 13–14.

2. Edward Rauff, *Why People Join the Church* (New York: Pilgrim Press; Washington, D.C.: Glenmary Research, 1979), pp. 86ff. It's noteworthy that friendliness can characterize a big church as well as a small one. One of Rauff's testimonies comes from a member of the Garden Grove Community Church in California, who says "everybody's friendly with everybody, because they don't know if they're visitors, members, or what. Plus they have small groups all week long" (pp. 87–88).

3. Ibid., p. 201. Other characteristics of "magnet churches" include vibrant worship experiences, attractive ministers, and programs which reach out and build up.

4. *The German Mass and Order of Service* (1526), in *LW* 53: 62–63.

5. Ibid., p. 63.

6. See my article, "Luther's German Mass: A Sixteenth Century Folk Service," *Journal of Church Music* 18 (October 1976): 2–6.

7. *LW* 53: 63–64.

8. Victor W. Turner, *The Ritual Process* (Chicago: Aldine Publishing, 1969), p. 126.

9. Martin Buber, *Between Man and Man,* trans. R. G. Smith (London and Glasglow: Fontana Library, 1961), p. 51.

10. Turner, *Ritual Process,* p. 129.

11. See the series of binary oppositions of liminality contrasted with status system in ibid., pp. 106–7.

12. See Richard Endress, "The Monastery as a Liminal Community," *The American Benedictine Review* 26 (1975): 142–58.

13. Nathan Mitchell, "Monks and Worship," *Worship* 50 (1976): 12.

14. Thomas Merton, *Contemplation in a World of Action* (Garden City, N.Y.: Doubleday & Co., 1973), p. 235.

15. Philip Jakob Spener, *Pia Desideria,* trans. and ed., with an introduction by Theodore G. Tappert (Philadelphia: Fortress Press, 1964), p. 90.

16. Thomas Merton, *Contemplative Prayer* (Garden City, N.Y.: Doubleday Image Books, 1969), p. 67.

CHAPTER 9

1. Frederic Debuyst, *Modern Architecture and Christian Celebration* (Richmond: John Knox Press, 1968), p. 24.

2. Edward A. Sövik, *Architecture for Worship* (Minneapolis: Augsburg Publishing House, 1973), pp. 18–19.

3. Robert Hovda, "Preparation, Formality and Style: Requirements of Liturgical Experience," *Living Worship* 9, no. 8 (October 1973).

4. Robert Hovda, *Strong, Loving and Wise: Presiding in Liturgy* (Washington, D.C.: Liturgical Conference, 1977), p. 40.

5. Rudolf Otto, *The Idea of the Holy,* trans. John W. Harvey (New York: Oxford University Press, 1958), pp. 69, 211.

6. See Frank C. Senn, *The Pastor As Worship Leader* (Minneapolis: Augsburg Publishing House, 1977), chapters 4 and 5.

7. Louis Bouyer, *Rite and Man: Natural Sacredness and Christian Sacraments* (Notre Dame, Ind.: University of Notre Dame Press, 1963), p. 84.

8. Royden Keith Yerkes, *Sacrifice in Greek and Roman Religion and Early Judaism* (London: A & C Black, 1953), pp. 25ff.

9. Alexander Schmemann, *For the Life of the World* (Crestwood, N.Y.: St. Vladimir's Seminary Press), p. 16.

10. Ralph A. Keifer, "Now the Sacred Words are Done: Liturgy in a Post-Translation Age," *Living Worship* 12 (May 1976).

11. See Gerald V. Lardner, "Communication Theory and Liturgical Research," *Worship* 51 (1977): 299–307.

INDEX OF NAMES

INDEX OF SUBJECTS